A
Flower
Arranger's
World

A Flower Arranger's World

DEREK BRIDGES

**Photography
by
Rosemary Weller**

CENTURY

London Sydney Auckland Johannesburg

To Sally Louise

Text copyright © Derek Bridges 1990
Photographs copyright © Rosemary Weller 1990
Illustrations copyright © Random Century Group 1990
All rights reserved

First published in 1990 by Random Century Group,
20 Vauxhall Bridge Road, London, SW1V 2SA

Random Century Australia (Pty) Ltd, 20 Alfred Street,
Milsons Point, Sydney, New South Wales 2061
Australia

Random Century New Zealand Limited, PO Box 40-086,
Glenfield, Auckland 10, New Zealand

Random Century South Africa (Pty) Ltd, PO Box 337,
Bergvlei, 2012 South Africa

Book design by Bob Hook
Editing and additional research by Susan Fleming
Illustrations by Catharine Slade

Set in Snell Roundhead Script and Bembo
Printed and bound in Spain by Graficas Estella

British Library Cataloguing in Publication Data
Bridges, Derek
A flower arranger's world.
1. Flower arrangement
I. Title
745.92

ISBN 0-7126-3755-9

Contents

INTRODUCTION

Flower arranging has opened up the world to me, and therefore it might be appropriate to elaborate a little on how I came to make my life within the world of flowers.

I never wanted to know exactly what I was going to be doing from nine to five each day, as you would in an office, and certainly couldn't conceive of doing it for 40 years or so. As I had always been interested in plants, a not so brief encounter 30 years ago with a flower shop in Halifax started me off. I then worked with the late Eleanor Shaw, a very well-known and brilliant teacher and demonstrator. I carried her buckets of flowers on to the stage, never dreaming that I would end up doing the same thing, never dreaming that I would be able to string more than three words together in front of an audience. When Eleanor retired, I started a flower shop with my wife Pat, and we soon realised that we might be able to do both – run the shop plus further my leanings towards flower-arrangement demonstration.

A collection of many of the bits and pieces used throughout the book – flowers, containers, accessories, spray paints, gourds, shells, chunks of glass, pieces of driftwood. My toolbox is there too, plus my scissors in the foreground where they belong – I can't do very much without these!

This we have done ever since, my techniques getting better and my audiences getting larger – culminating in 1979 with more than 3,000 at the Opera House in Blackpool.

I demonstrate mostly to flower clubs the length and breadth of the United Kingdom, many of them members of NAFAS – the National Association of Flower Arrangement Societies – which celebrated 30 years as an organisation in 1989. (Many individual clubs, however, have been going for much longer than that, some for at least 40 years.) It was through NAFAS that the germ of the idea that became WAFA – the World Association of Flower Arrangers – was born. Founded ultimately in 1981, in Great Britain, WAFA had the aim of establishing and maintaining contacts between flower clubs and societies throughout the world. Founder members included many of the countries featured in the following pages, and one of the first decisions taken was to give one individual country a mandate to oversee the Association for three years. In June 1984, the British stewardship of the Association culminated in a world conference in the beautiful city of Bath. I was delighted to be associated with this show, not only as a competitor, but also as a teacher. A magnificent festival three years later, in Brussels, saw the end of the Belgian reign – and brought even more countries into WAFA. Paris is the venue for the show being organised by the French in June 1990.

I have had the good fortune – and honour – to be able to benefit extensively from the facilities WAFA offers, and in recent years have visited many of the WAFA countries – among them Kenya, South Africa, Malta, the USA, Belgium, Australia and several islands in the West Indies – and have participated in many international festivals and competitions. It is in tribute to this – to the work of WAFA in promoting a single language of flowers throughout the world – that I have conceived and written this book. It is not in any sense an official WAFA book, but I hope that by revealing my individual reactions to, impressions of, and ideas concerning each country belonging to WAFA, the value of an organisation like WAFA can be more fully appreciated. There are also many countries whose interest in flower arranging is so extensive that they too ought to be members of the Association. A shared love of flowers can help overcome many barriers, whether linguistic, cultural or political, and long may it do so.

I began by saying that flowers had opened up the world for me. That is literally true, and flower arranging has turned me into a seasoned, competent and happy traveller. I've seen how flower arrangers in countries like Malta – where there is little vegetation – can really use their imaginations to overcome those limitations, coming up with spectacularly original ideas. I've seen how an ingredient which is exotic to me – a palm spathe, for instance – can be thought of as too commonplace to use in the land of its origins. In Trinidad, for instance, I'd polished some spathes beautifully to use in an arrangement, but couldn't take them with me; when I offered them for free, no-one moved – at home I'd have been mown down in the stampede! I've seen the amazement on some faces when I use fruits and vegetables in arrangements, but why not when they're as much plant material as anything else?

What I've seen and appreciated most of all on my travels are ideas which have inspired me: whether abroad on holiday or working, I spot things, keep them in my mind, make notes perhaps, and then blend them with my own ideas into something that is uniquely me. Travelling to all points of the compass – north and south, east and west – constantly furthers and expands my interest in and knowledge of the art of flower arranging. As I have recently learned that a flower club has just opened in Moscow, who knows, one of my next ports of call might be the Kremlin!

THE BASICS OF FLOWER ARRANGING

Whether you're flower arranging solely in your own country or, like me in this book, are 'travelling' around, using ideas and materials from elsewhere in the world, the first thing you'll need to organise is some basic equipment. It's like taking up cooking. A cook can't hope to produce interesting dishes with just one pan, half a bag of flour and no sugar; to make a cake properly you first need all the correct ingredients. It is exactly the same with flower arranging, and just one or two items of equipment are the first necessities.

Tools of the Trade

I think it essential that you buy yourself a good pair of scissors and secateurs. My scissors have been with me now for about ten years, and I almost can't start thinking about anything until they are in my hand. You also need a good strong sharp knife, but this doesn't mean the old kitchen knife you no longer want to use in the kitchen!

The other thing I couldn't live without is my toolbox – one of those mechanics' little plastic toolboxes with swivelling layers, lots of little compartments, a handle and a lid. This can take the scissors, secateurs and knife for a start, but it will also take all the *other* things you'll begin to collect – the paper clips, drawing and safety pins, cocktail sticks, skewers, sticky tape, sticking plaster, nails, hammer, etc. These may seem remote from flowers but even the briefest of looks through some of the arrangements in this book will open your eyes to what is actually needed. Whenever I go to a show, someone's sure to lack something and say, 'Oh, Derek will have it in his box'. I probably do but it's really time some of them had their *own* well-filled boxes after all these years!

The other thing I think you'll find really useful is florists' wire in various lengths and gauges: a bundle of each of 30-gauge silver wire and a 22-gauge 'blue' wire should see you all right.

Mechanics

These are the absolute basics of every flower arrangement, the bits and pieces that hold the flowers in place. Floral foam is the most important, and this comes now in a multitude of shapes and sizes. It cuts simply into any shape you require too. It must be soaked before any fresh plant material is inserted – about 10-15 minutes in a bucket of cold water – and then kept wet in the arrangement. Keep it wet too in a plastic bag, if you want to use it again in another arrangement for, once dried out, you can't resoak it. There is also a drifoam which is used for dried flower arrangements. Floral foam tape will hold a block of foam securely in a container.

For extra security, pinholders are often needed to hold the floral foam, and these come in various sizes. And for even weightier or taller arrangements, pieces of wire netting or chicken wire are useful: mould them over the top of the foam like a hairnet.

Containers

Ideas for collecting containers could take up a book in themselves, and I've written exhaustively on the subject in all my other books. One of the most important things, though, is not to start collecting containers that are too *small*. It may be a beautiful little figurine, but if the bowl is too small, three flowers will fill it and the arrangement won't last.

It's difficult for me to advise on how many or what kind of containers you need. I've been collecting for years, and I still say that if anything will hold floral foam or water then it will take an arrangement, whether it's a chipped Victorian tureen or a plastic bowl. The list is endless, and again a quick look through the book will open your eyes to many more possibilities – a simple glass sugar bowl, a half coconut shell, a straw hat, wicker ring or basket, a wooden box, even a concrete garden birdbath! To come down to absolute basics, though, the containers I use most often are plastic tubs or boxes such as might have held yoghurt or margarine: these slot in quite a few places and hold enough foam for many arrangements. Pieces of driftwood make lovely containers too, as do shells. You can also *make* containers, and there are a few ideas here (but many more in *The Crafty Flower Arranger*, my last book).

Bases and Lifts

I think bases beneath a container can improve the setting of an arrangement, making the whole thing more of a 'framed' picture. They must always be in harmony with the container and the ingredients of the arrangement, and there is quite a selection of bases in the book. I've used slices of wood, pieces of slate, a mirror and vitreolite tiles, trays in various colours and small wooden or bamboo tables. I've also *made* bases, covering pieces of fibreboard carefully with fabric to tone in with the arrangement. Lifts can be created in much the same way - by covering tins, boxes or rolls of cardboard with fabric or paper.

Backings

All the photographs in the book were shot in a little outhouse at home in

Yorkshire, and against different types of backings (hanging paper, fabric, canvas, etc). A photographer's trick perhaps, you might think, but backings certainly have relevance to the flower arranger who is interested in competing. Just as a base can form a frame at the foot of an arrangement, a complementary backing can really show off an arrangement to its greatest potential. In domestic terms, you wouldn't dream of setting up an arrangement against a busy wallpaper where it would be lost; you'd arrange it against a plain backing where every detail of your creative input could be seen and appreciated.

In the Korean arrangement on page 69, for instance, we hung some linen behind where the arrangement was to be shot, and then sprayed it with various spray paints to give a complementary muted, almost shadowy, background. The backing for the main Japanese arrangement is a slatted bamboo screen to echo the bamboo base and container; that for the step-by-step arrangement is a Japanese painting.

For the American step-by-step arrangement on page 39, I created some hanging wall drops to complement the decorated ring. Not strictly a 'backing', but near enough. These were made from stiff cardboard cut slightly less wide than the ribbon (about ¼ inch/1 cm each side) and then the gold-edged, silk moiré ribbon was glued on. (Do make sure

that the glue is in a dryish state or it will ooze through the ribbon.) The bells I used come whole but I cut them through the middle to make a half-bell shape. They are from China, the cleverest things I've seen in years; a fibreglass base covered with layers of real pine-cone 'scales', tapering up in size, to create an almost Chinese roof-tile effect. Groups of the same material as I used in the ring were glued to the top of the bell halves, working both in tandem (as you would any two-part arrangement). To complete the effect, I added gold silk tassels to pick up the gold edge of the ribbons and, to cover up the joins, two tiny little cones.

Other Accessories

I have been collecting containers and accessories for flower arranging now for over 30 years, and I think if I let some flower arrangers loose in my three converted lofts, they'd have a field-day. I will not throw anything away, knowing from experience that I'll find a use for it some day, whether by itself or nailed, bolted or glued to something else. I'm always saying that I haven't been beaten yet when it comes to an object that looks unlikely. However dubious you think an offering from a friend might look, *never* turn it down: the next thing he or she offers you could be a treasure. This has happened to me so many times.

The sort of things I mean are the

bits and pieces you pick up in jumble sales, in a car boot sale, at the side of a road, in a skip – quite a few of the ingredients in the Italian arrangement on page 117, for instance. Or the things you might pick up when on holiday – the lovely Spanish basket, the wooden triangles, a grain scoop from Africa and a beer strainer (a beer strainer?). You might bring back a bronze lamp from the East, or a hand-thrown pottery bowl from the West – both can probably be used in some arrangement or another. Accessories can also mean those items that you've collected together in another sense – old books, boxes, *objets d'art*, etc.

Into this category too must come the artificial glitter, baubles, spangles and beads, icicles, wooden fruit shapes, painted wires, silk flowers and foliage, etc, all of which are available in floral accessories shops, and which are absolutely vital for arrangers at Christmas – *the* time for every flower arranger, especially me.

Candles are accessories too, and they require special thinking. If they are thick, they will need a tripod which can be pushed into the floral foam (thicker candles would split the foam). Tape three wooden skewers or saté sticks around the sides of the candles, half the skewer length protruding below the bottom of the candle. These 'legs' then push into the foam and hold the candle firmly. If you like the dripped wax candle effect, see page 114 for some ideas as to how to achieve this. More than anything, though, I urge you to use candles that are *long* enough. There is no point in having candles as a major feature or accessory in an arrangement if all you see is the little white wick poking out above the plant materials in the arrangement. The candles are there to give *light* as well as atmosphere, and should always be seen.

Other accessories are bits of driftwood, shells, etc, and their use requires a little advance preparation. Most wood pieces that you want to bring indoors have to be cleaned first so that you don't introduce any bugs. Swill and scrub them with a bleach and water mixture and then dry thoroughly. Shells too might retain creatures - as well as a 'smell' – so put them in a bucket of paraffin for a week before rinsing thoroughly in water. This tip was given to me by some friends in Kenya – travelling *does* broaden the mind and extend knowledge!

THE BASIC INGREDIENTS OF FLOWER ARRANGING

Once you're equipped with your basic tools of the trade, and have started on your collection of containers, bases, lifts, backings and accessories (it's endless, I warn you), perhaps it's time to think about the basics of the art, the plant materials themselves.

Conditioning Plant Materials

Whether a plant grows naturally in your garden, or it's an imported species that needs special attention, or you're actually picking plants in their exotic native habitat, the first thing it needs when cut is a good long drink. Every single plant, whether native or exotic, needs this basic conditioning before it can be used in an arrangement. The floral foam for arrangements *does* hold water, of course, but it can't hold *enough* to fill the stem of the flower with water – which is what conditioning is all about.

Whether at home or abroad, pick plant materials in the early morning or late evening, *never* in the heat of the day. As soon as anything is picked, particularly in a hot climate, evaporation of natural moisture begins. Take a bucket of tepid water *with* you into the garden, and put the plant stems straight into it. Cut the stems at a good sharp angle to give a larger area into which water can be taken.

Place individual flowers or foliages in individual buckets of water so that you know how many and how much you are picking. Never *over-pick*, because what you leave on the tree or plant is there for you to pick *next* time. Even if you're faced with the most lush of foreign gardens, where there seems to be more vegetation than anyone could ever miss, you should remember the *economics* of picking.

And, before leaving the flowers to condition for at least 12 hours in a cool place, take off any lower foliage or leaves. This will stop the water becoming foul.

When I was in Natal, I was introduced to the idea of taking all the foliage off flowers like bougainvillea and submerging the flowers completely in water for a couple of hours. This did seem to work there, but it might not for *all* types of plant.

Most plant materials can simply be picked and then conditioned as above, but some need special treatment. Woody-stemmed plants need to stand in about 2 inches (5 cm) of boiling water for about 20 seconds, then placed in deep cold water for 12 hours as above. Some plants with stems which exude liquid – euphorbias and helleborus, for instance – need to be singed: hold the cut stem end over a flame until scorched and sealed, and then plunge into the 12-hour conditioning water as above.

I've used a lot of house plants in this book, and they too need 'conditioning'. Remember to water as appropriate, spray those that like it from time to time, and, the best tonic of all, put them out into the garden during the summer. They'll love it!

There are some tips and hints about individual plants in the Plant Glossary at the end of the book.

Preserving Plant Materials
A great deal of the plant material I use in the arrangements in this book are preserved in some way – usually dried but some have been glycerined. Often this is the only way in which one can enjoy the glories of other countries' plants, by bringing them back dried or to dry.

The easiest way of drying is to pick and simply hang your materials. Pick, at home or abroad, during dry weather, just as the flowers open or when a seed head begins to ripen and turn brown. Hang in a dry airy place and most things will be ready in about four weeks. Some plants – like proteas

and hydrangeas – actually dry well *in* arrangements once the foam has been allowed to dry out.

There are a few tips on materials that can be dried in the Plant Glossary on pages 126-43.

Glycerining plants makes them less brittle when 'dried' than other dried materials. It's particularly useful for branches of foliage and leaves like beach, eucalyptus, oak, box and laurel, and aspidistra, camellia and moluccella. Put a mixture of two parts very warm water and one part glycerine in a tall container; it must come up at least 2 inches (5 cm). Mix well and stand the stems of the plants in it. Leave in the cool and dark for anything from three days to six weeks, or until the plants have turned colour, usually to a cream or golden brown.

Once you've dried or glycerine-preserved your plant material, store it *very* carefully as it's delicate. Use florists' long boxes if you can get them, and separate with wads of tissue paper. They will then be clean, dry, protected and ready for virtually instantaneous use in arrangements whenever fresh plant materials are scarce.

Collecting Plant Materials
If you're a serious flower arranger, you're a serious collector, and every time you go abroad – whether on holiday or, like me, to work – you'll see plant materials that you want to

take home. I'm not talking necessarily of fresh plants, but of all the bits and pieces like seed pods, palm leaves and bracts, date palm bracts, and gourds. Always take several plastic bags with you into which things can be collected while you wander along a beach or through a tropical plantation.

To bring them home, you could of course buy another suitcase, but I always take with me an empty florists' box which packs flat in my suitcase. I fill it at the other end, tie it securely with string and then, on the way home, send it through with my other pieces of luggage. I'm always prepared, and if you enjoy travelling as much as me, I advise you to try to do the same.

Happy hunting!

Africa

Africa is known as the Dark Continent, christened thus because its hinterland was largely unknown until as late as the end of the nineteenth century. It is the second largest continent after Asia, and consists mainly of high plateaux which drop dramatically to narrow coastal plains. Many of the continent's rivers – the Nile, Zaïre (Congo) and Niger are among the ten longest in the world – leave these plateaux in magnificent and spectacular falls, some of the features most familiar to Africa lovers and visitors. Two-thirds of the continent lie within the tropics – the equator bisects Kenya – and although temperatures are always modified by altitude, Africa is the hottest continent, as well as one of the driest – a fact brought tragically home to us in recent years by the drought and famine in Ethiopia and other countries.

The climate and vegetation of Africa vary considerably from the arid desert of the Sahara in the north – which covers 25 per cent of the total area of the continent – to the tropical rain-forest of the Congo basin, and south of the tropic of Capricorn to South Africa. In countries of the Mediterranean or sub-tropical north like Morocco, there are fertile valleys and enough moisture to grow vines; the wines of South Africa from the equally sub-tropical south are now known the world over. In between, as well as desert, there is savannah, covering another 40 per cent of the land. Most of the soil is poor, but there are rich pockets of vegetation and agriculture on the East African highlands, in the alluvial river valleys, and in the plains beside the sea.

Many of the plants of Africa have adapted because of the climate, and have become characteristic of the continent. Some have leathery sepals or thick woody stems; these help in drought conditions. Succulents are common too, plants which have fleshy stems and/or leaves that function as water storage containers. Divided leaves help reduce water loss, and hairy or shiny leaves help minimise the harmful effects of intense sunlight.

It is the *profusion* of plants and vegetation in Africa that I love most. Having now visited quite a few African countries, both professionally and for pleasure, two of my favourites remain Kenya and South Africa which are members of WAFA. The flower arrangers there are full of ideas and use to the full the wonderful things that Mother Nature has produced for them. They too use the dried spathes and fresh or dried leaves of palms;

they too make use of gourds, fresh or dried, of the bracket fungi, and the driftwoods bleached white by the sun (although they would probably use aloe branches found in the veldt, rather than pine), as well as the wealth of flowers and foliage, many unique to the continent. Because most of that African profusion is available to us only as house plants, however, I have chosen to feature some of my favourite dried plant materials – to me not dead as many people claim, merely 'resting'. Along with a few examples of colourful fresh lushness, the arrangements on the next pages sum up what Africa means to me.

KENYA

Kenya is in East Africa, lying across the equator on the Indian Ocean. It is bordered by, to the north, Sudan and Ethiopia, to the west by Uganda, to the north-east by Somalia, and to the south by Tanzania. The fertile south-west highlands are Africa's major source of tea and coffee, the country's main exports. (Others include sisal and pineapples.) In the north lies Lake Turkana or Rudolf, in the Great Rift Valley where so many important fossil hominoid remains have been found by the Leakeys in Olduvai Gorge. Kenya is also famous for its big game reserves, among them Tsava National Park.

I have been to Kenya four times now, each trip as delightful as the last. There used to be two flower clubs there, one in Nairobi, a smaller one down in Mombasa, but sadly the latter now no longer exists. My first trip to Kenya was many years ago, only the second time that I'd demonstrated abroad. It was a tremendous challenge to me, setting foot on foreign soil with nothing other than my travelling tool kit as I obviously could take no containers, accessories or bases with me. (What I took *back* with me is another matter!)

I was absolutely enthralled by my drive from the airport into Nairobi because the sides of Kenyatta Avenue were emblazoned with jacaranda trees in full bloom. These, curiously, come into flower first – a most intense blue – followed by the fern-like foliage and the wonderful seed pods. That was my first impression of Kenya.

I was staying with members of the Flower Club, and my next impression was of their magnificent gardens. This lushness is the result of the climate, quite rarefied, as Nairobi is 6,000 feet (1800 metres) above sea level. For instance, I saw sansevieria, or mother-in-law's tongue, growing like grass along the edge of paths. There were wonderful palms, bananas and bougainvilleas, as well as poppies and delphiniums (*D. macrocentron* grows particularly well in the Kenyan highlands).

In the streets of Nairobi, flowers were sold from stalls on the pavements. Among lovely tropical things were the omnipresent delphiniums, larkspur, African marigolds, and foliages in bunches (which I didn't need, as I'd raided everyone's gardens by then). There were also the native fruit and vegetables – everything from pineapples and mangoes to oranges and grapes, and many things I couldn't even identify – which I chose to use many of in my arrangements. On my first trip this intrigued the members more than anything else!

The flower-arranging club in Nairobi has now been going for over 25 years, and it is a marvellous blend of people and races, all working well together and sharing a tremendous interest in flowers. I remember the first time I went there I had to get used to the heat above all, but the flower club ladies were very well organised: the dems were always held in a lovely cool hall and began at approximately 4 pm after tea at 3, when it's cooler and much pleasanter for them, for me and for the flowers. (Incidentally, cutting flowers in a hot country requires even more consideration and care, so turn to page 13 for some ideas I've culled from my travels.)

In between my two weeks in Nairobi I was given a weekend off which was very nice. The first time there I went on a safari very near to Mount Kenya. On another break, I went to the Mount Kenya Safari Club which was started by the late William Holden. A few thousand feet up the slope, in a beautifully laid-out garden where crowned cranes strut majestically, you can have a delicious dinner then sit on your veranda with a view of the snow-capped, moonlit peak in front of you and a double brandy in your hand. Many say paradise has been lost, but in my opinion paradise was there.

On yet another occasion, I went to Lake Naivasha with the Horticultural Club of Nairobi to visit a carnation farm, reputed to be the world's largest. They employ 3,000 workers who grow the flowers from cuttings, pick them and send them off three times a week in jumbo jets to the markets of the world.

On one of my Kenya visits, I went to Mombasa as well, taking the most wonderful train overnight, which meandered its way those 6,000 feet down to sea level. I thought Mombasa was wonderful, as I love the sea and beaches, particularly beautiful there. There are magnificent shells, corals and pieces of driftwood, but we are not allowed to collect these now. (For tips about cleaning beach finds such as these, see page 12.)

On my last visit in 1988, I was very pleased to see that the Nairobi Flower Club was flourishing again after a few hiccups. The hard-working committee, for whom no little job was too much trouble, deserve full credit. I will never forget how much they did to make my visits a success, nor their amazing hospitality, and I hope it is not too long before I set foot on Kenyan soil again.

Kenya is one of my favourite countries, not only because of the friends I have made, but because of the wealth of stunning vegetation. To many people Kenya will probably mean safaris and savannah, with little but palm trees and monotone scrub, but around the major cities, such as Nairobi itself, there are some of the most beautiful and colourful private gardens I've ever seen. This arrangement then, is a combination of all those elements.

The main features are the two enormous double palm spathes sweeping to left and right. These spathes – or spoons as they're sometimes called – are the bracts on the stem of the palm from which the new leaf develops: they fall off or are cut off as the palm grows in height. I used them point down into a heavy container holding soaked floral foam, which sits on a bleached-wood base. These spathes did in fact come back with me from one trip to Kenya, and I wanted to use them as they look almost like carved African masks to me. In the centre of the arrangement, as spine height, are two woven wicker tubes: these are local beer strainers, and the idea is that you put the liquor plus various bits and pieces into them, and what drips through into your glass is meant to be drinkable. (I'm only using them as accessories: I wouldn't try imbibing the contents!)

To the right of the grouping, I've placed a selection of various dried gourds – very visually exciting in their myriad shapes – and to the front, an interesting piece of driftwood.

For fresh foliage material, I've used cordyline as spine height. I've inserted sprays of nephrolepis fern with, to the right and front, leaves of monstera – in Africa, a climbing vine plant, to us a sturdy but useful house plant. White anthurium lilies bring their colour and dramatic shape to both sides of the grouping. These are known also as flamingo flowers and, although white, not the red variety, could be said to represent the bird life of the country. At Lake Nakuru you can see up to 3 million flamingos at one time!

Tucked underneath are some fresh pineapples: these were introduced to Kenya in the early part of this century and are now grown in enormous quantities. Ananas plants, the decorative pineapple tops, are the main feature at the centre of the arrangement. These can be bought as a house plant, and are very useful to use in a decorative manner because of their lasting qualities. The two ananas I use in my dems were put in the garden in the hot summer of 1989 where they very kindly produced for me the two babies used here! One last touch was the echeveria popped into the top of the shorter beer strainer.

I think there's a nice feeling of Kenya here – the dryness, the local accessories, the fruit and the flamingo flowers (anthuriums).

SOUTH AFRICA

South Africa is made up of a narrow coastal plain rising sharply to an interior plateau flanked by the Drakensberg Mountains which sweep along the whole eastern side of the country. The north-west part of the country includes the southerly tip of the Kalahari desert. Thus South Africa itself, let alone Africa, is a country of contrasts.

There is a wealth, though, of material growing there, much of it indigenous. Proteas, of course, are the most famous South African flower, and the official floral emblem of the country is the giant protea, *P. cynaroides*. Members of the *Proteaceae* family vary enormously: they can be tiny, or trees like *Leucadendron argenteum*, the silver tree. Protea growing and exporting is now a major South African industry.

However, South Africa is also the original home for many other plants which have become familiar to us. Pelargoniums or zonal geraniums are native, as are strelitzia (bird of paradise flowers), belladonna lilies, gerberas and zantedeschia, the arum lily. Another lily, the nerine, is also native, and *N. sarniensis*, the Guernsey lily, acquired its name after a ship bearing bulbs from the Cape to Japan was wrecked near the island which thereafter took enthusiastically to

cultivation of the flowers.

Other plants seen in abundance are the Livingstone daisies (*Mesembryanthemum criniflorum*) which carpet the veldt in the spring, bougainvillea, azaleas, bottle brushes, bush lilies, Hottentot figs, gladioli, red-hot pokers (kniphofia), as well as all the wonderful foliage plants like maranta, monstera, croton, sansevieria and yucca, all known to us mainly as house plants. South Africa has, in fact, contributed enormously to the development of modern forms of many plants: gladioli, geraniums, freesias, strelitzia, gerberas, kniphofia, agapanthus and nerine.

It was with great delight that I accepted an invitation to go to South Africa in 1981, to do a tour starting at Johannesburg, then to Durban, Port Elizabeth and Cape Town. I arrived in Jo'burg and I went to the Chairman's house to have tea in her garden – in February, I may add. I was staggered to see in the same flowerbeds spring flowers and daffodils with beautiful blooming roses, all the seasons together! That was my first real introduction to the flora of Johannesburg.

From Johannesburg I travelled to Port Elizabeth on the Indian Ocean coast. My hostess there, again the Chairman of the local flower club, took me to the Botanical Gardens.

This was where I first came across cycads growing, some I'd never even heard of. I wasn't allowed leaves off any of the rare or protected cycads, only the common ones. The rare ones were literally chained down in concrete blocks as they'd had one stolen a couple of years before. (Worth thousands of pounds, it had ended up in a garden on the other side of the world.) There I saw aspidistras growing almost like grass, the tallest I'd ever seen.

The next port of call was north, to Durban, a more tropical city, again on the Indian Ocean. For my main picking I was taken to the magnificent garden of Rosemary Ladlau. There were golden Livingstone daisies, day lilies, Queen Elizabeth roses, and a profusion of proteas and leucospermums growing on a sunny hillside.

I had been asked to go and demonstrate down country in Natal, by some friends from Kenya who had retired to a coastal town called Ramsgate (quite different to that in Kent!). I had to transport all my containers, flowers and so on from place to place and it took a fleet of four or five cars. The team of ladies who re-conditioned the plant materials were wonderful and, thanks to them and despite the heat and humidity, all the plants and the demonstrator (their first from overseas) travelled and survived magnificently.

Sadly, because of time, I could not travel by train to Cape Town, and flew, missing out on the wonderful Flower Route. To my delight, I was able to pick in the world-famous Kirstenbosch, the headquarters of the National Botanic Gardens of South Africa, and home to the most comprehensive collection of the South African *Proteaceae*.

Another aspect of Cape Town amazed me. Flowers are sold on street corners, out of old cleaned oildrums, by farmers and growers from up country. In these magnificent arrays was everything I needed, be it gladioli, carnations, roses, leucospermums, proteas, goldenrod, or bunches of sweetpeas. No demonstration preparation could have been easier.

A little extra treat was to come, a visit to the garden of Jocelyn Stewart, a very well-known Life Vice-President of NAFAS. She had emigrated from her famed garden in Norfolk, England, to the outskirts of Cape Town where, to the surprise of many, she had directed her energies to creating a new garden from scrubland. It is, I would say, the most magnificent garden of its size in the country.

The kindness of the people, the friends I've made, the beauties of the country and its flora, made my trip to South Africa one of the supreme highlights of my flower-arranging life.

I have gathered together here a collection of tropical dried materials, to represent my reactions to South Africa. Most of the ingredients were brought back from my wonderful trip there. As many of you know, I have a tremendous love of dried plant materials, and what I most like about what I've used here is the fantastic contrast of textures: although the colour scheme is limited to brown and tan, the textures of the various leaf shapes and flower surfaces create tremendous interest.

The base is a slice of wood, on which sits a heavy metal stand with a container where the main part of the arrangement is. The stand was also useful in that I could attach the very large palm spathes to it: they are wired into holes in the metal cup at the top of the stand, the middle one hiding the mechanics of the bottom two (see the Kenya arrangement for details about these spathes). I sometimes use the spathes flat, as containers themselves, but I like to rear them up in this way to get all that rhythm and movement. (You'll need space for this – the finished arrangement is over 6 feet/1.8 metres tall.)

To the top of the arrangement there are two further palm spathes, which are inserted into drifoam in the container. I've slightly polished these to highlight and bring out the colours. To the right, the next placements were curls of eucalyptus bark which had fallen off a huge tree. When I gathered it, it was already beginning to curl, but I encouraged it even more (see page 133). These curls sit in the drifoam as well, and create more wonderful rhythm and movement.

To the left-hand side there are some clipped cycad palm fronds. These were green and whole when I gathered them but as they started to 'go over' I clipped them into these spear shapes; they're very useful in many arrangements, either for height or, as here, in a sweeping line to the side. The next placements were the wonderful many-fingered palmetto palm leaves above the cycad spears. These can be gathered in many countries, and stay green for a very long time before eventually drying. Above these are two placements of a very interesting dried material, bagged from a large bamboo in a friend's garden in Africa (see page 128). Some other palms, clipped into a shield shape, sweep out to the right.

And, of course, no South African arrangement would be complete without the proteas, the focal point here. To a lot of people this arrangement may look rather drab, but I urge you to study it and try to see what I see and feel what I feel – the undeniable interest and wonderful textures of this type of plant material.

A brown and tan arrangement to represent South Africa, which uses many dried materials, including the wonderful protea flower.

1 The base of the arrangement is an African grain scoop made of plaited wicker, which I brought back with me from one of my trips. This holds the soaked floral foam which I secured on to a spiked holder because of the immense weight of the materials. The first placements are decorative calabash gourds, one whole dried one to the left, another cut in half lengthways to show the wonderful scoop shape towards the front. These are used as ladles in Africa.

2 I've invoked my artist's licence here by using a wonderful piece of fasciated contorted willow – not a tree native to South Africa – but to me, if that doesn't look like the antlers of some veldt antelope, I don't know what does!

3 To help tidy off the mechanics, I have used a piece of dried flat fungus with, flowing to the front, a cluster of fresh gourds highlighted with leafshine. These, as well as the calabashes, are now quite easily available in flower shops but try to collect some on your next trip abroad to exotic climes! (Dry them well, see page 132.)

4 The foliage part of the arrangement is created with croton leaves and this further hides the mechanics. Croton is a very useful house plant indeed, you can take off the odd leaf and the plant still keeps going. (It's used as hedging in South Africa.)

5 Two stems of 'Enchantment' lilies bring their singing orange into the grouping, echoing the tones of the variegated leaf and of the gourds. The final touch – the talking point, vital to every arrangement – is the cut fresh gourd, showing the wonderful seeded interior.

A combination of dried and fresh material which, for me, speaks very loudly of its origins, the colours, textures and shapes echoing those of the savannah in that wonderful country, South Africa.

The
Americas

The Americas are named after Amerigo Vespucci, an Italian navigator who explored in South America in the late fifteenth, early sixteenth centuries, discovering the mouths of the Amazon and Rio de la Plata. It was of course Christopher Columbus who, a little earlier, discovered the West Indies and North America. Unusually for his time, he believed the world was round, and that it must be possible to reach the east by sailing to the west. He landed in 1492 in what he thought were the East Indies, in reality of course, an island in the Bahamas: later voyages led to the discovery of Puerto Rico, Jamaica and Trinidad. The islands between the massive land masses to north and south duly became the West Indies – although they're nowhere near India!

Together the two major parts of America, with some 28 per cent of the world's land, approach Asia in continental size. Despite their teeming millions though, the Americas are inhabited by only just over 25 per cent of the population of Asia (think of the sparseness of population in the north of Canada, and the vast uninhabited peaks of the Andes). From north to south, the Americas stretch some 9,500 miles, more degrees of latitude than any other continent. This, in flower-arranging terms, makes it rather difficult to generalise about the country, as it encompasses so many climatic zones as well as so many different cultures. From the polar north of Canada to the humidity of tropical Mexico, and the sea-dominated islands of the Caribbean – not forgetting Bermuda – the foliages and flowers vary enormously, as do the styles of the flower-arranging art.

It is from North America, however, that most of the influences come, and one of their major and most creative seasons – as it is or should be for every flower arranger – is in the winter, at Christmas. Anybody who has had the pleasure of being in the United States at that time will agree with me that the American ideas are absolutely fantastic. They decorate their trees magnificently (see page 31, in the introduction to my Canadian arrangement), and they extend a sense of festivity in so many wonderful ways.

One is the welcome ring, one of those such as I used in the step-by-step pictures for the USA, but suspended from the door. It still upsets and surprises me that so many people in this country don't do this. It's a welcome to your guests before they even ring the bell, and I love the glow on faces before even stepping across the threshold. These rings are available in the British Isles now in many guises, ranging from bent coathangers bound with mosses, to bound twig rings, many of them coming from the Far East or Canada, straw or Spanish broom (the latter from Spain). Neither do they need to be used exclusively at Christmas; it's the ingredients you decorate the ring with that dictate its mood.

In seasonal arrangements the North Americans excel as well, using natural plant materials with artificial – a combination I'm always urging on my students. They might use artificial poinsettias, ribbons and baubles, of course, but amongst them they will have wonderful cones, lichen-covered branches, dried seed pods and pieces of fungus to bring in that natural look.

Not only do North Americans

love rings on their doors, but they also often make and drape garlands around doors, going to town as we've seen in so many Hollywood films of the old days (when they really *did* make films). Think of *White Christmas*, for instance, when they did as much decoration outside as they did inside. These garlands could also be made for inside, to wind over a mantelpiece, to hang around doors, or to snake up a staircase. These too can be brought out at different times of the year, depending on the ingredients you use.

It's the travelling that I do that inspires me, introducing me to new ideas, new concepts, new uses of material. Having been lucky enough to visit many parts of the Americas, I've culled some wonderful inspiration from the vitality, resourcefulness and spirit of their varied peoples. It's one of the greatest excitements of my job, the continual learning process, and I love it.

CANADA

Canada is the second largest country in the world, occupying the entire northern half of North America (except for Alaska, on the north-western tip). Its vast size encompasses six different time zones, ten provinces, two territories – the Northwest Territories and Yukon Territory – and two main languages, English and French. (There are also the languages spoken by the original inhabitants of the country, the Indians and Eskimos.) To the west of the country, the Rocky Mountains hug the Pacific coast; between these and what is known as the Canadian Shield, lie the interior lowlands which mainly consist of prairies and plains. The south-east holds the Great Lakes – through which the Canada/US border passes – and the main population areas of the country, in the great cities of Toronto, Ottawa, Montreal and Quebec.

The great size of Canada means there are many different types of climate. The very north is polar, and there is little vegetation, not much scope for flower arrangers! South of that there is *taiga*, a Russian word for the great areas of cold coniferous forest that stretch in an immense belt from Siberia around Asia to Alaska; here there are long winters and short, warm summers with little rainfall. These forests of pines and firs, so characteristic of the country, cover more than a third of its land mass, and as a result forestry has long been an important element of the Canadian economy. The height of the Rockies makes for a temperate climate band on the east Pacific coast where Vancouver is situated; there is also a large temperate zone in the east around the Great Lakes and the length of the St Lawrence River. The Rocky Mountains also screen the land to the west from the moisture of the ocean, creating the dry grasslands or prairies, which stretch south from Canada, through into the mid-west of America, the traditional lands of cattle and maize.

So, although I haven't actually been to Canada, either as a tourist, or to demonstrate, my main impression is of a vast, mainly unspoiled country with long cold winters, short summers, and forests of magnificent trees. These include the unique Douglas fir (*Pseudotsuga*), discovered first by a Scots member of Captain Vancouver's voyage of 1792, and then named later after another intrepid Scotsman, David Douglas, envoy of the London Horticultural Society, and the sugar maple (*Acer saccharum*), which is the emblem of Canada.

Because of these trees, particularly the conifers, it's rather appropriate, I think, to talk about how they're used at Christmas, a time so lavishly and splendidly celebrated, in flower-arranging terms particularly, in the whole of North America. It was there several years ago, that I got the idea of Christmas trees being decorated in one colour, an idea I now constantly emphasise in my demonstrations, in my classes, and in my books. Although many think this could be uninteresting, it's not, and in my opinion, it's much more effective than the normal gaudy selection you might see in this country. I once went into a North American bank, an old one with a magnificent foyer entrance and galleries, and the Christmas tree there must have been 45-50 feet (13-15 metres) high. It had artificial snow on its branches, looking so real that the tree could have just been transplanted from the Rockies and the snow somehow petrified. (A common mistake made by people is spraying their tree with artificial snow in such measly quantities that it looks as though a Christmas bird rather than a snow cloud has just passed overhead!) That was a white and silver scheme,

but other trees might be decorated all in red – bows, lights, parcels, baubles, the lot. In a North American hotel with a permanent decor of blues and greens, their trees were decorated in toning colours, and the effect was absolutely stunning. One of the best trees I've done myself was an artificial blue-green spruce decorated with tones of ice-blue and glass and crystal. So, although your Christmas tree might not come from the Rockies, take a leaf out of the Canadians' book, decorate it subtly and selectively, and sit back and wait for the compliments.

I have met quite a few Canadian flower arrangers despite not having visited the country. Although I've heard that they are as enthusiastic there about flowers as I am, and that they can grow most of the same sort of flowers as we do here, I still feel that the coldness dominates, that there are times when fresh material is much less available than it would be here. This is why I have chosen to use mainly dried and artificial ingredients in my arrangement to represent Canada. One day, who knows, I may be able to go there and see for myself!

I think of Canada as a country of contrasts, the forest wilderness in the uninhabited parts quite different from the sophistication of her beautiful cities. I also think of Canada as a modern country, so chose to represent her in quite a stylised modern arrangement. There's a hint of Christmas here in the use of glitter and velvet, and no fresh material; the colourings are cool - but not *too* icy or cold – to represent the mountains, snow and winter sports image.

Sitting on a silk-covered circular base are two ceramic blue containers, one on a lift. Don't ever think, when using containers like these, that you have to fill them with floral foam – that would be a waste. I managed to find two cream cartons that very nicely wedged into the top of each container, and these took the drifoam. (The lift, by the way, is a baby food tin which I've covered in the same fabric as that used on the base. This is a very easy way in which to create different levels in an arrangement such as this, and also to achieve that feeling of togetherness.)

When using two containers in the one arrangement, always work them both together so that you can get the balance correct. Here the height is created by the arrangement in one container, with the width divided more or less equally between the two, but with echoing concepts to create the all-important visual links. The height was created with fine fronds of glittered reed and dried yucca leaves which I'd spray-painted a blue-bronze. These foliages also created the width to left and right. Weight is added to the height and both sides of the width with sprays of grey-blue frosted plums.

To add other shapes, and to give the all-important rhythm and movement to both areas of the arrangement, I twisted some of the glittered reeds into circles and inserted them in the drifoam. Two very useful rings, covered in a velvet in the same grey-blue colour, were added to the foam at the right of the top arrangement.

To add weight towards the centre of both arrangements, I used some clipped palmetto palm which again I had painted in a complementary colour. A bow of toning silk moiré ribbon in both arrangements gave another dimension and texture. All that was needed now was for the central focal point to be completed, and for this I used groups of artificial grapes and apples, in bronze and frosted grey-green colourings.

A cool modern arrangement representing my image of Canada, and which would look wonderful towards Christmas. The idea can, of course, be adapted for any other time of the year.

THE UNITED STATES OF AMERICA

The 48 states which make up the bulk of the United States - excluding Alaska and Hawaii – form the most populated and fourth largest country in the world. Like Canada, it is bordered to the west coast by the Rocky Mountains, and also by the Pacific mountain system: this latter runs roughly along the fault in the earth's crust responsible for those earthquakes in California, around San Francisco in particular. In the east of the country, the Appalachians extend north from Georgia to Maine, on the border between the US and Canada. Between these ranges lie huge plains.

Again like Canada, the vastness of the country encompasses many climatic variations. The west and a part of the north-east is temperate on the whole, and the centre is dry grassland – the grain bowl of America, and where the buffalo used to roam. Around San Francisco there is a pocket of what is called Mediterranean climate; this is characteristic of coastal regions that lie between a temperate zone and a desert – for not too far distant is the aridity of Death Valley (and indeed the western border with Mexico). In Florida and the Deep South, there is the sub-tropical climate so beloved by sun-starved holidaymakers.

Thus anything goes in America as far as vegetation is concerned, and after the New World was discovered in the late fifteenth century, the Old World took to many of its plants with gusto. This was when American plants such as tobacco and potatoes were introduced to Europe. (The latter actually originated in South America, Peru to be precise, but arrived in Britain via the colony of Virginia.) Later, the great plant collectors and botanists explored the length and breadth of the USA and Canada. One of the first was the young John Tradescant who went three times to Virginia and was responsible for introducing a great number of trees and plants to the UK and Europe. By 1656, the Tradescants' garden in Lambeth boasted many of the most striking of North American trees, for instance – the robinia or false acacia, the tulip tree, the swamp cypress and the eastern red cedar. Another garden was stocked with North American plants at Fulham, by the then Bishop of London. And it was the association between one Peter

Collinson, a London draper and plant enthusiast, and John Bartram of Philadelphia (the first native American botanist, whom Linnaeus described as 'the greatest living botanist in the world') that directly led to the foundation of the UK's greatest botanic garden, at Kew. The list of plants native to the United States, and which have since become familiar to us in Europe, is almost endless: it includes Michaelmas daisies (called Tradescant's aster), goldenrod, lupins, witch hazel trees, the balsam firs, lobelias, carnivorous plants such as Venus flytrap, gourds, pumpkins and squashes, etc. The eighteenth century was the greatest era of European gardening, the exploration of North America quite amazingly accelerating the extent of European botanical knowledge. We've not looked back since.

I have actually demonstrated in the United States, in New York, where John Tovey and I presented our 'Food and Flowers for the Four Seasons' a few years ago. I had met many Americans on holiday and socially, but had never demonstrated to them before, so didn't know quite what to expect. After I started my part of the session – when I try to use everything that is seasonally available, flowers, foliage, fruit, vegetables, dried materials, you name it – I was rather taken aback by the silence, the lack of response. I don't expect them to interrupt, of course, but I do tell

some quite nice stories while I'm doing my stuff, and usually there's a bit of laughter. It wasn't until I got to about the third arrangement that a rapport seemed to be appearing – and I later discovered it wasn't until then that they'd got used to my lingo. I do, I must admit, talk rather fast!

After that, I relaxed, they relaxed, and it all went very well. The audience was mixed – some had come for the food, some for the flower arranging, and some I imagine had come in just for the sit-down – and I was interested to hear some of their comments afterwards. The general reaction seemed to have been how different my style of floral art was to the normal style in the States. I was able to point out how I like the challenge of utilising all the materials that are available then and there in the countries to which I travel, as well as how uninteresting it would be if we all thought and acted in exactly the same way when it came to flower arranging.

Thus I chose to represent the United States with one arrangement speaking to me of the modernity, almost brashness, of the country – using accessories, ideas and colours in a typically Bridges way – and another which is more traditional, a decorated ring to celebrate perhaps the all-American festival of Thanksgiving.

In comparison with Europe, the United States of America is a New World, and I wanted to capture that newness, that modern feel, in an arrangement to represent my reactions to that vast country.

My accessories here are glass bricks, which can be obtained from plumbers' merchants, especially those that deal in bathroom and shower fittings. They make wonderful containers and accessories, especially here, where I've used them to give the feel of those modern skyscrapers in many American cities that tower up, consisting of nothing, it seems, but glass. I fixed these together securely and placed little containers holding soaked floral foam at the three levels (use Blu-Tak, wire, anything that will hold everything in place).

I also wanted a vibrant rhythm and movement throughout the arrangement so, because I like to incorporate as much natural material as possible, I chose to use some rattan cane that had been dyed a wonderful blue. It's easy to handle, and I wired whorls of it together and pushed it into the foam at all three levels. The wonderful rhythm sweeping from left to right was created simply by other lengths of the cane: at the top, pieces were pushed into the foam, then were curved round into the middle arrangement foam; two more pieces swirl out into the bottom arrangement.

As America has such a huge variety of plant material, I was uncertain at first what to use. However, skyscrapers are condominiums, blocks of apartments, and so I thought the idea of using foliage from house plants was relevant. The height, though, is created by rye grass, here the lovely flowering seed heads plus some of the strip foliage. To give depth to the back of the rye grass, I used sprays of camellia foliage. People *do* have these as house plants, and not only are the flowers magnificent, but the leaves make wonderful foliage for flower arrangements – strong texturally and visually, and they are one of the longest-lasting foliages when cut. To add lightness I used one of my favourite indoor plants, the nephrolepis fern, which sprays out at the sides of the three groups. Other prominent foliages are the wonderfully variegated leaves of fatsia, and sprays of the invaluable canariensis ivy.

The flowers had to be white – the clouds in the blue sky to which the skyscrapers reach? – and these are carnations, snowberries, and *Gypsophila paniculata* (this double flower variety known in the UK as Bristol Fairy, and in the US as baby's breath).

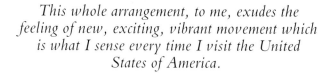

This whole arrangement, to me, exudes the feeling of new, exciting, vibrant movement which is what I sense every time I visit the United States of America.

Thanksgiving is a very North American celebration, taking place in the USA on the fourth Thursday of November and in Canada on the second Monday of October. Ring arrangements have long been traditional at this time, but more as welcoming door decorations. They can also be used flat, though, as here, as a table decoration - a good idea for Christmas too, especially with the complementary hanging bells.

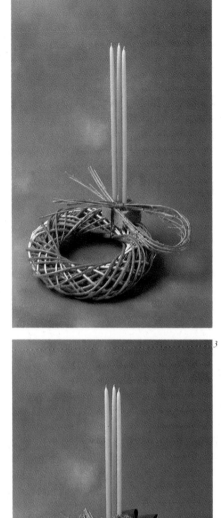

1 A piece of drifoam was attached to the stripped willow ring with floral foam tape. The first placements were the three slender candles: these were pushed into the foam just as a flower stem (thicker candles would need a tripod, see page 12). Anchored in place in the foam with a double stub wire stem is a twisted wicker bow.

2 To the right of the candles, the next placement was a double bow made of chocolate brown hessian and cream pleated paper ribbon. (You buy this ribbon as twisted paper cord, then unravel it, when it opens up into lovely pleats rather like Fortuny dress fabric.) Then comes the foliage, artificial blue spruce to left and right with, as a complete contrast, artificial velvet-surfaced brown ferns and glossy sprays of enamelled leaves.

3 Some wood leaves – wood as thin as veneer cut into leaf shapes with a stem glued on – were added. Then, to start the fruity, harvesty effect I wanted, and to get another contrast in shape, I placed in some dried African bean pods and bunches of bronze-green artificial grapes.

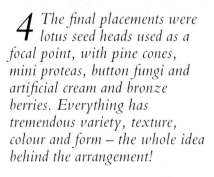

4 The final placements were lotus seed heads used as a focal point, with pine cones, mini proteas, button fungi and artificial cream and bronze berries. Everything has tremendous variety, texture, colour and form – the whole idea behind the arrangement!

5 To complement the completed ring, I made two wall drops, using cardboard, ribbon, tassels, two half-bell shapes, and some of the same ingredients as used in the ring (see page 11). A wonderful way in which to celebrate Thanksgiving – or indeed Christmas – just change the ingredients.

MEXICO

There are many flower-arranging societies in other Central and South American countries, but Mexico is the only one which belongs to WAFA. Mexico is a country of Central America, lying between the Gulf of Mexico and the Pacific Ocean. It is bordered in the north by the USA and in the south-east by Guatemala and Belize. Most of the country is mountainous, three-quarters of it lying above 1,500 feet (450 metres); the Sierra Madre ranges enclose a high central plateau which is very earthquake prone. Mexico City, the capital, sits at the southern end of this plateau, not too far from the volcanic Popocatepetl. Much of the north is arid, and far too dry for agriculture, while there are tropical forests in the south, especially in the Yucatan, the low-lying peninsula to the south-east.

Mexico, more than any other country in the Americas perhaps, is steeped in history. Today the majority of its people are fairly poor, relying on the farming of maize, so it is difficult to remember that the whole tongue of land between North and South America was once ruled by great and advanced civilisations: the Olmecs in about 5,000 BC; the Mayans between the second and thirteenth centuries AD; after them the Toltecs until the twelfth century;

and from the fourteenth, the Aztecs. The latter based themselves in the city of Tenochtitlán, the site of the present-day Mexico City, until they were defeated and destroyed by Spain under the command of Cortes in 1521. It was from these voyages of conquest that the Spanish brought back to Europe many of the unknown foods which have become so familiar to us in the intervening centuries – tomatoes, maize (corn), green beans and lima beans, avocados, vanilla, chocolate, turkeys and the characteristic Mexican peppers, ranging in potency from the very smallest and fiercest to the large sweet red and green varieties.

Mexico is rich in botanical history too. Many plants are native to the country or were discovered there – the echeveria, the zinnia, the fuchsia, the dahlia and the begonia. Plumier found one type of the latter there in 1690, and named it after a French botanist called Bégon, then the governor of Santo Domingo. One of the best-known and loved of our pot plants, the poinsettia (*Euphorbia pulcherrima*) was discovered growing wild in Mexico by a Dr Poinsett; it was first shown at an exhibition in Pennsylvania in 1829 under the name of *Poinsettia pulcherrima*, the relationship to the euphorbias not having been recognised. Other plants growing there are the usual tropical delights such as palms, cacti, heliconias and anthuriums.

I haven't yet visited Mexico properly, either going there as a tourist to stay, or visiting as a demonstrator. I have met and watched Mexican flower arrangers though, and they do brilliant and vibrant work, as exciting and visually noisy as the market I visited when I went on a brief trip across the border from California. This is what I hope I have captured in my own arrangement representing the country.

When on holiday in California with my wife Pat and daughter Sara, we decided to visit Mexico. We drove down to San Diego after a hefty breakfast: we'd been warned if we couldn't boil it or peel it, not to eat it! We left the car on the US side, went through the border post where two traffic lanes led into Mexico, and strolled about three-quarters of a mile to the little town of Tijuana. It was market day, and I can truthfully say that I have never before seen such confusion! Everything was noise, colour, profusion, smells, and people swarmed everywhere, typical of any Latin market. Sara clung to my arm all the time, not her sort of place at all. There were wonderful arranged displays of the produce they use in the cooking – chillies, aubergines, tomatoes – and stalls cooking and selling food. One woman I watched was making tortillas – the thin pancake the Mexicans eat like bread, made from ground corn – on an upturned oil drum with fire underneath it. She poured on the batter, let it sizzle, then turned it over, quite probably trapping several of the flies that swarmed everywhere!

Another thing that intrigued me was the church, set in the middle of the square. The services went on continually, and it wasn't even a feast day. It was rather like going to the cinema, you could watch the end of one show and the beginning of the next! Church-going was as frantic as the rest of the market: people came in on their bikes, parking them at the end of the pews, then doing their thing; prams were wheeled in and blocked the aisles equally successfully. There were some lovely flowers there, but I couldn't help thinking that there was room for a few classes and a bit of tuition on how best to use the 550 peach and red gladioli that shouted colour from every corner.

We left Mexico reluctantly because it had been so exciting, but fairly swiftly as we were so hungry. Our egress was helped by the fact that there are no fewer that 22 lanes *out* of Mexico into the US, but hampered rather by our British passports which I insisted on having stamped. We raced to a Californian restaurant where we enjoyed their version of a Mexican meal!

My visit was hardly enough to get a true impression of the real Mexico. However, the country means colour to me, tremendous vitality and excitement, so that is what I have chosen to represent in this arrangement here. I also had one or two things which I thought were in keeping – the first of which is a real Mexican hand-thrown pot, which I acquired recently. This I filled with a collection of various fruits and vegetables – aubergines, peppers of all hues, tomatoes – the sort of things one might find in the richest of Mexican chilli dishes.

On one of the steps I placed a large plastic bowl, filled with two blocks of soaked floral foam as the materials to be used were quite heavy. To create the height at the top of the arrangement, I used a plant material I very much associate with Mexico, the pampas grass. It's been dyed in reds, oranges and yellows to start off the very vibrant colouring of the group. The large palm spathes have been spray-painted inside in the same red and orange colours to link with the grass. It almost looks as if the grass were emerging from its 'bud', with those toning colourings.

Coming in from the lower left, we have some wonderful large sea grape leaves. These grow all over the Caribbean, beside the beaches, and are now used by almost every flower arranger as a flat leaf. They have been dyed a lovely sort of ochre, again to link in with the various colours of the arrangement. Ferns and more palm spathes provide other textures and shapes to the sides, and the flowers I've used are gladioli, spray carnations, carnations, 'Mercedes' roses and dahlias, all the sort of things that I think would be grown in Mexico and which continue that vibrancy of colour.

To further complement the arrangement, I placed behind and to the side of it, two large natural woven mats, and a jug (such as might hold tequila?).

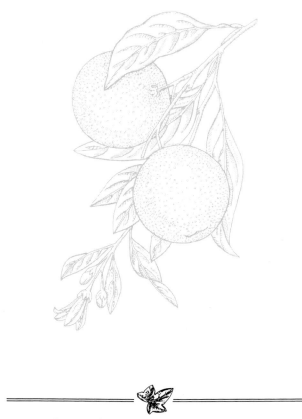

On the rough stone steps against the equally rough stone wall (actually an outhouse at home), the grouping looks as though it might just be in an adobe dwelling down Mexico way at fiesta time.

My second Mexican arrangement looks, I think, rather as though it's part of a rain-forest habitat, with epiphytes growing in the clefts of the tree branches, or a fruiting cactus in the dry scrub.

1 A very interesting upright piece of pine driftwood, about 3½ feet (1 metre) high, is used as the main feature, standing, slotted neatly into another piece, on an orange lacquered base. There were two convenient nodules at bottom right and top left which took containers holding soaked floral foam. *Begonia rex* leaves hide the mechanics.

2 Working both arrangements together, I placed in whirls of cane, lovely spirals which had been soaked, tied and dried in the same way as the eucalyptus bark (see page 133) to create the corkscrew effect. Preserved sea grape leaves were given wire stems and made into sprays sweeping out from both sides of the arrangement.

3 Further foliage pieces were added – the lovely bright orange-spotted croton leaves and the dark green pointed leaves of the spathiphyllum. To give a much more delicate effect I used the slender foliage – not the flower plumes – of the pampas grass. (Handle this with care as the edges are razor sharp.)

4 The outline had now been created with a combination of fresh and dried materials. Pineapples were anchored in the arrangement at top and bottom, using the tripod method (see page 12), three kebab or saté sticks pushed at one end into the pineapples and then the other end into the floral foam. To give a third dimension to the arrangement, and to prevent the pineapples looking far too dominant in each area, I used the lovely starburst centres of the cordyline.

5 The final additions at the base of the arrangement are the wonderful and interesting shapes of cup and saucer gourds or squashes. The orange and green striped effect links up with both the foliage and the pineapples, and with the orange lacquer base we started with.

Islands Around the Caribbean

The islands of the Caribbean are of many sizes and shapes, with distinct geological origins. Different 'wings' of the curve of the West Indian islands were formed at different times and in different ways. In the first great series of earth movements that formed mountains – over 70 million years ago – the volcano backbone of Mexico and Central America appeared: one branch of this chain extended eastwards to what is now Jamaica, another branch to southern Cuba, Hispaniola, Puerto Rico and the Virgin Islands. In the south the Caribbean coastal range uplifted, stretching through Colombia and Venezuela to Trinidad, and possibly to Barbados. A little later the volcanic islands on the north-east of the curve were formed and became inactive. In the second great mountain-building episode, the volcanic islands of the Leeward Islands, on the inner westerly side of the curve, were formed on the upslope of the first curve, so these islands are much higher than their easterly neighbours. Intermittent volcanic activity still occurs in the Lesser Antilles, and the strain on the earth's crust is revealed by thankfully infrequent tremors and earthquakes.

The different geological origins of the islands have engendered very different habitats. Those which are low have little rainfall; those which are volcanic in origin – such as Martinique and Dominica - can be so high that there is a frost at night. On some islands, the height of the mountains creates rainfall which means rain-forest, tropical epiphytes, bromeliads, ferns and mosses; on some lower islands, where there is less rainfall, savannah and grasses predominate. Along the fringes of most islands, coconut palms grow on the beaches, being immune to the effects of salt; further in on the coastal plains there is often cactus thorn scrub or sea grapes and other bushes, permanently bent low through the force of the sea breezes.

The one consistency of the many islands is the uniformity of the temperature – a fact known and enjoyed by many of us rain-sodden folk of Europe. There are two seasons – one which is rainy, and the other which is fairly dry – but it's always hot.

In the days when European countries fought over and claimed individual islands, the British West Indian Islands were thought of as 'the jewels in the English crown'. I just think they're jewels, and I'm very fortunate to have visited them.

BERMUDA

I have included Bermuda in my section on America because it is situated 600 miles to the east side of the North Carolina coast, although it is actually a self-governing, and Britain's oldest, colony. I have also included it with the Caribbean islands although, being some 1,000 miles north of them in the Atlantic, and on a similar latitude to Madeira, it has much gentler average temperatures – ranging in the winter from 65-70°F (18-21°C), and in the summer from 70-85°F (21-29°C). The climate is sub-tropical, warmed by the Gulf Stream, but there is no real rainy season.

Bermuda actually consists of over 150 small coral islands, many now joined together by causeways and bridges. The largest is Bermuda or Great Bermuda; others include Somerset, Ireland and St George. It is altogether just 22 square miles in area, and is fringed by pale pink coral sand. Discovered by a shipwrecked mariner, Juan de Bermudez, in 1503, it was over a hundred years before the islands were claimed for Britain by Sir George Somers, in 1609. Amidst the exotic sun, sea, birds and the prolific hibiscus, oleander and bougainvillea, this Britishness still reveals itself in traditional afternoon tea and in a force of British bobbies – although they do wear short trousers!

Various things bear the qualifying word 'Bermuda', some more likely than others. The Easter lily, a variety of *Lilium longiflorum* that blooms around Easter, is also known as the Bermuda lily, and exports of bulbs to the USA is another island industry. There is a Bermuda or wire grass used in warm countries for lawns, a Bermuda cedar, a Bermuda rig for yachts and – of course – Bermuda shorts!

The other, more sinister association with the name of Bermuda is that infamous triangle – the 3 million kilometres of water between Bermuda, Florida and Puerto Rico. Those same earth movements that raised the islands of the Caribbean also created enormous trenches in the sea bed. The Brownson Trough north of Puerto Rico and the Virgin Islands is over 29,700 feet (9,000 metres) down, deeper than Mount Everest is high, and is the deepest part of the Atlantic Ocean. This great depth, and powerful air and sea currents circling in the area, are thought to contribute to the number of ships and aircraft lost, and to the lack of wreckage.

However, my image of Bermuda still persists – of sun, of sea and sky, all blues, greens and tranquillity – and thus my main arrangement is designed to reflect this feeling. My other Bermudan arrangement reflects quite another aspect!

I think of Bermuda as a beautiful island surrounded by blue sea and blue sky, and that was the atmosphere I wanted to create in my representative arrangement.

When planning a seascape such as this, something which represents the sea, either under it, or beside it, you must *think* sea. A lot of people slip up by putting in various objects or flowers that never, in a million years, could be thought of as having a connection with the sea. The shape, formation and *feel* of all potential seascape ingredients must be considered very carefully.

Looking through my collections of bits and pieces, I discovered what I use here as the central spine height. Looking like seaweed fronds wafting their way up towards the surface of the sea, they are in fact the empty fruiting 'branches' of the date palm: when the tree fruits, these hang down, laden with luscious fresh dates. They are tremendous even in their natural dried state, but I spray-painted them lightly with various tones of turquoise, blue and green to give me that coral, undersea type feeling.

These date palm bracts are placed in a sturdy container holding drifoam, and set on a piece of slate from the Lake District (not Bermudan, of course, but has the right bluey-green colouring).

The next placements are the fans of sea fern which come to both left and right of the arrangement. This can be collected on many beaches around the world, but particularly in the Caribbean (where they use smaller pieces as sauce whisks!). Again they're beautiful in their natural state, with a coral-bronze colouring, but I gave them a light bluey-green application of spray paint to echo the arrangement colourings.

Wandering through the arrangement, on various levels, are some of my collection of shells. These, too, can and should be collected from beaches all over the world. They're wonderful used as accessories in flower arrangements, and very decorative in other ways too. It was the colour of these shells – particularly the ones called peacock's ears (they make good soap dishes at the side of the bath) – which originally determined the colours of the arrangement, as they catch the light in such an exciting way.

It is very difficult in this type of arrangement to know which type of flowers or foliage to use, because they must look sea-like - roses, gladioli or carnations would be completely out! So I have gone for cut echeverias in one tone or another: some lovely big green ones, and some smaller in tones of blue-grey or silver grey. They could almost be sea-urchins . . .

Although I haven't yet visited Bermuda, I conceive of it as an island dominated by sea and sky, and thus I have gone for a cool blue seascape.

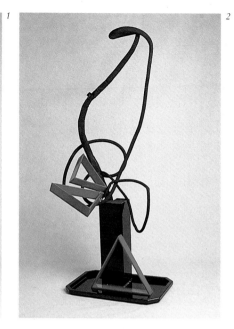

To contrast with the muted tones of the other Bermuda arrangement, I wanted to be dramatic and modern, to echo the undoubted brightness of that lovely island.

1 *A tall black acrylic container – an umbrella stand, I think – was placed on a black acrylic tray. I wedged in blocks of floral foam to the level of the container, but next to a piece of 1½ inch (4 cm) plumber's grey pipe at one side of the container. This was used because it was needed to keep dry one of the ingredients, the lovely black whirls used as height, which is a worm-like seaweed, very appropriate to an island like Bermuda. This has hardened into this state, but if it got wet it would soften again, so this is why I used the grey pipe to makes its own individual container. I could then soak the surrounding floral foam properly. The seaweed is hollow so I cut a little cleft into the top thicker sweep into which I could wedge a plastic test tube to take water and the intended top part of the arrangement.*

2 *The second placements are these triangles of scarlet-painted wood, a lovely addition to any arrangement, but here particularly useful because of the different shapes created. These I bound together to have a sturdy wire leg to anchor into the foam.*

3 *I did not want anything to detract from or disguise the seaweed, so I used small sprays of a very interesting foliage,* Gaultheria shallon. *This flows to the right of the lower arrangement to balance the curves of the seaweed, and sits in a curve in the tiny top container.*

4 *To intensify the scarlet colour of the triangles, I used red carnations for my flowers. There is a low cluster only in the bottom arrangement, again so that the basic stark and dramatic shapes of the seeweed were not hidden.*

5 *As a final touch, I placed a couple of red carnations in the tiny top arrangement, and a third red triangle free-standing on the tray. With an echoing triangle of light coming in on the background, looking rather like Concorde taking off, did I hear someone mention the Bermuda Triangle?*

BARBADOS

arbados lies rather by itself in the easterly part of the curve of the West Indian islands, probably formed by the same upsurge that produced Trinidad. Generally low-lying except for a part of the north-east, it is a beautiful, once British, island, which has been a fully independent state within the Commonwealth since 1966. It was first discovered by the Portuguese and gained its name from the banyans which once heavily wooded the island. These trees, known locally as the bearded fig (*Ficus citrifolia*), have suspended aerial roots which the Portuguese likened to beards, thus *Los Barbados*, the bearded ones.

Barbados is not a member of WAFA, but there is a very enthusiastic flower club there. This was the first club I visited in the Caribbean, and I am very proud to be an honorary member of it. They elected me during the AGM on that first trip after I had given my impressions of my visit. The major thing I noticed was that they all seemed to prefer using imported flowers like gladioli and roses – everything, including the flowers I needed for my dems, coming in from Miami – and were actually shunning the prolific and wonderful local plant materials apart from the odd anthurium, ginger lily or heliconia. I suppose it might be a case of , because they *live* surrounded by these beautiful plants, thinking they're too commonplace. Anyway, this comment from me elicited a couple of sniggers but I persisted, saying that if they were kind enough to invite me back, I hoped to see a difference.

Invite me back they did, and I *could* see that difference. In just two years, the ladies had opened their flower-arranging eyes, and were using materials from their gardens and from the hedgerows in wonderfully imaginative ways. I applauded all of them enthusiastically, and presented them with a trophy to be awarded at their annual show in November to the arrangement making the best use of local plant materials. This trophy, a walnut carriage clock, has now been won twice, and I like to think of it sitting on a mantel somewhere in Barbados, a reminder of the times I'd been there and had impressed them slightly!

TRINIDAD

Trinidad is a large island off the coast of Venezuela, and, united with the smaller island of Tobago, it became the Republic of Trinidad and Tobago in 1976. Inhabited firstly by the Arawaks and Caribs, it was a Spanish colony from the sixteenth century until 1802, when it was ceded to Britain; Trinidad and Tobago formed an independent state in the British Commonwealth from 1962-1976.

It is not primarily a tourist island, which I find surprising as it is so beautiful. Neither is it a member of WAFA, although there are some very enthusiastic flower-arranging clubs. I have been to the island a couple of times (sadly, not yet to Tobago), and I always remember my first impression of the wonderful hills, the wild vegetation, and the magnificent plant material in my hotel garden in Port of Spain. The trip had been organised by the flower clubs of the island and the Girl Guides Association, both of whom were to share the profits if any (these were considerable, I believe).

The Guides provided their headquarters the first time as a venue, which was not exactly ideal, but the demonstration was a success. The second time the venue was different, they told me, but *how* different! The Bank of Trinidad had built a new head office, part of which was a most magnificent hall with tiered seating and a fantastic stage with lighting and curtains. The demonstration was a success, and the manageress even asked if I could leave the flowers on view for the locals.

I went on to San Fernando, again to a Girl Guides HQ, but what a contrast with the hall I'd just left. This was a hall the size of a tennis court, with a concrete floor and no windows, just open space at the sides. On hearing that there were at least 400 people coming I was nervous about them being able to see. 'Don't worry, we're building you a stage,' I was told. Duly, but not until the junior school closed at lunchtime, this 'stage' was erected – using 48 schooldesks (thankfully flat, not sloping). Having first checked that I was insured, I tested them out, and I slid to and fro, feeling a bit like Torvill and Dean. I expressed more worry, and the remedy was to tie all the legs of the desks together with string. After covering the 'stage' with black material, and assembling all my bits and pieces, it looked quite effective. The dem went well too, to the biggest audience they'd ever had in San Fernando. It all goes to prove that, whatever the situation, we flower arrangers have to think on our feet.

JAMAICA

Jamaica – whose name is derived from the Arawak word *Xaymaca*, land of wood and water – lies in the Caribbean Sea off the south coast of Cuba, and is almost in fact like two islands, the western two-thirds fairly 'flat', rising to the heights of the Blue Mountains in the east. It was discovered by Columbus in 1494, and occupied by the Spanish who exterminated the Arawak population; it was captured by the British in 1655 and became a colony and a centre for the slave trade. In 1962 Jamaica became an independent state within the British Commonwealth.

At the height of its colonial days, at the beginning of the nineteenth century, Jamaica was producing about 100,000 tonnes of sugar per year, and this, including the by-products of molasses and the best rum in the world, is still a major export. Coffee is another major crop, and grows well in the hills: the cooler climate there causes the berries to ripen more slowly, and they develop substances which, on roasting, give the coffee its flavour. Blue Mountain coffee costs the earth, but is quite delicious. Bananas are grown there too, and the palms give good shade for young cocoa and coffee plants. In amongst the coconuts, bananas and forest-clearing clumps of heliconia, to my immense surprise were masses of azaleas. These were apparently taken out by British settlers, and went wild; although they're not British in origin, the glowing purple and pink clouds beneath the exotic palm fronds did give a British sort of feel to a tropical landscape.

Jamaica is a garden island, with a floral abundance all year round. The vegetation is huge because of the tropical climate, and far too big for flower arranging. Some of the palms had fronds on them about 15-16 feet (4-5 metres) across, and unless you were decorating a cathedral, not very much use! (In fact, they're used there dried for some of the bird tails on their carnival costumes.) There are poincianas, gold cassia, yellow pui, bamboos and begonias in the mountains and, in December, it almost looks like a giant Christmas card with carpets of pure white euphorbias contrasting with their red cousins, the poinsettias.

The symbols of the island are blue mahoe (a hibiscus), the flower of the *Lignum vitae* tree, the doctor bird, one of the smallest in the world, and the akee. This is an intriguing fruit, and was named *Blighia sapida* after Captain Bligh who brought it to Jamaica along with breadfruit from West Africa in 1778. I thought they looked fantastic, with a reddish-orange skin which opens up like a flower when ripe to reveal three black seed-eyes peering at you. Only the white bit round the seeds is edible and must be eaten at exactly the right time: if under- or over-ripe, it is very unsafe. I tried saltfish with akee, the local dish, and it was quite delicious. The fruits, though, were good to use, mostly at the base of arrangements, as were breadfruits, like green hedgehogs, local mangoes, pawpaws and pineapples, a never-ending list of goodness. I also used Job's tears (*Coix lacryma-jobi*), a weedy sort of grass which has attractive shiny fruits often used as beads in jewellery (and rosaries and local bead curtains): they're pale green-blue and grey in colour, dry very successfully, and I use them a lot at home in dried-flower arrangements. (The grass is also a cereal and fodder crop, with good food value as a flour, apparently.)

I spent most of my time in Kingston where I demonstrated. On this side of the island it's mainly industrial, the biggest business being the exporting of bauxite, a mineral mined from the limestone of the 'flat' side of the island, and from which is extracted aluminium. But I had the opportunity to go across the island on my days off to the holiday resorts of Montego Bay and Ocho Rios. Coming down into Ocho Rios, there is the wonderful Dunn Falls, water cascading over a fantastic rock formation: it was raining when we

were there, but in good weather you climb up, hand in hand, in your bathing suits with a glass of something thirst-quenching to help you along. I also managed to get permission to go and see the late Sir Noël Coward's house and garden. How inspired he must have been by the view from his study – over a beautiful garden, over the sea, almost to the horizon. Everything was just as if he'd popped out for a minute, a piece of music manuscript on the piano, pen nearby, and his clothes laid out on the bed. He's buried in the garden, in a favourite spot for entertaining, with a wonderful gazebo over him.

It was on my way home to Kingston that we stopped at the roadside stalls for barbecued corn on the cob. They literally hook them over the fire, coat them with butter and hand one over wrapped in a tissue. Delicious is not the word for it, and another of the lingering memories of Jamaica.

Visiting Jamaica was another highlight of my flower-arranging life. Not only is the island tremendously interesting and quite beautiful, but the enthusiasm of the local flower arrangers is very infectious. Jamaica, to me, means wonderful colours, a fusion of vegetation and fruits, and the sense of being on an island surrounded by sea. This is what I've tried to recreate in my arrangement.

Because of the very heavy weight of the materials, I needed very strong mechanics. A heavy oblong pottery dish sitting on a large hessian-covered base took two whole blocks of soaked floral foam covered with wire netting. The first placements were the pieces of lightly stained bamboo: these give the framework height, and echo the 'jungles' of bamboo growing in the Jamaican hills. Suspended from the top of the bamboo is a naturally hollowed-out coconut shell which I found when wandering along a Jamaican beach. This holds some soaked foam and three anthurium lilies. Giving that interesting red ladder effect is the heliconia, one of the most dramatic flower formations that can be seen in many parts of the world, particularly the Caribbean and Africa. The one here is the hanging type, *H. marginata*, which literally suspends in this form, and is normally bright scarlet with yellow edges. This one was dried and then spray-painted a soft red.

Sitting at the bottom of the arrangement, I have my representation of the sea and Jamaican fishing, a crab and lobster. They were given to me by my friend Bobbie who had used them fresh in a still-life in a Yorkshire flower show: they had to be removed as, before too long in that particular part of the hall, we began to get rather a whiff of the sea! She had them treated (I know not how), and they must now be about 20 years old.

Then I chose to represent the fruits of the island: to the left a melon, some glorious yellow courgettes and orange peppers; to the right an aubergine, a mango, a hand of bananas and peppers, gradually coming in towards the centre with a couple of those delicious Jamaican corn cobs.

For final placements, I used three more anthurium lilies, and, centrally, the large leaves of the sieboldiana hosta: the variegated leaves at the side are *Fatsia japonica*. The pièces de resistance here, though, are the great pinaa shells, enormous fan shapes in a lovely browny terracotta colour, again given to me by Bobbie.

Enclosed in a virtual bamboo jungle are the flowers, fruits and colours of that garden island of the Caribbean, my representation of Jamaica.

Asia

Asia is the largest continent, occupying about one-third of the dry land of the world. It ranges from the Urals in the west (dividing Asian Russia from European Russia, Europe physically being a peninsula of Asia), across the bulk of the land mass to the Pacific in the east. It is bordered in the north by the Arctic Ocean, and in the south by the Indian Ocean. Asia also includes the south-eastern islands of Indonesia, Japan, Borneo, Taiwan and the Philippines.

Asia is a continent of great diversity, containing both the highest point in the world – Mount Everest in the Himalayas – and the lowest, the Dead Sea. It has been of enormous importance historically – all the religions of the world were born in Asia, for instance, and many of the greatest civilisations. Botanically, it has been of great value too, for many of our favourite trees, shrubs and flowers in Europe are of eastern origin. Sir Joseph Banks, when director of Kew Gardens, sent plant collectors all over the world, many to Asia: one of them was William Kerr, who sent back the tiger lily and the water lily. Later Sir Joseph Hooker brought back many rhododendrons from the Himalayas. Robert Fortune's booty included honeysuckle, chrysanthemums, jasmine, weigela, forsythia, mahonia and skimmia. Ernest Henry Wilson discovered a lily, a dogwood, a maple, a clematis, a buddleia, and some 50 or so azaleas. Even at the beginning of this century many new species were still being discovered. There are probably a few still waiting.

Japan and Korea are the Asian members of WAFA, neither of which, sadly, I have visited. But I have been to other parts of Asia, namely Hong Kong and Singapore, both of which are fascinating places.

I went to Hong Kong to demonstrate to the local flower club, and stayed in the Hilton Hotel where I was also performing. Although many might think that Hong Kong consists only of skyscrapers, it's really very lush once you get on to the mainland or over the peak. One day during my trip in 1988, I was taken to wonderful flower areas where they were cultivating in the old traditional ways – the ladies bent double, wearing black hats with fringing. I was there during the run-up to Chinese New Year, when peach trees and the mini orange trees called kumquats bring good luck and prosperity for the year to come. In the Hilton, the whole foyer was decorated with these plants, and the aroma was quite spectacular.

The Hong Kong Flower Club ladies were raising money for their charity of that year, the Kidney Trust of Hong Kong, and I demonstrated in the ballroom of the Hilton in front of 600 people. I went to the local flower market, a densely packed area of little streets and lots of stalls, which offered everything from orchids to carnations. I got foliage there, as well as from various gardens – yucca, aspidistra, palms, ferns and sansevieria. I also was generously loaned some astoundingly beautiful containers.

In Singapore, I was just a visitor, en route back from Australia. There is a flower club there, I know, but the whole place is a flower arrangement in itself. In the airport there was the most wonderful build-up of driftwood with dendrobium or Singapore orchids, sitting like butterflies on the branches. In our hotel, we had a welcome bouquet of orchids, and two arrangements to match the decor, one in the bedroom, one in the bathroom. When we came back from dinner, there was a spray of orchids on each pillow with a lovely home-made chocolate and a message saying 'Sleep well'. Pampered is the only word for it!

My experiences of Asia have been nothing but good so far. I look forward to more.

JAPAN

Japan is a country in east Asia consisting of a series of islands lying between the Pacific Ocean and the Sea of Japan, the latter separating it from the land mass of Asia. The four main islands are Honshu, Hokkaido, Shikoku and Kyushu, all mountainous, with the highest peak, Mount Fujiyama on Honshu, rising over 12,000 feet (3,500 metres). The Japanese islands lie on the Pacific 'ring of fire' as do the islands of New Zealand, so are prone to earthquakes. The climate of Japan is maritime temperate on the whole, with good rainfall, the cold sea current from the north (the Oyashio) offset by the Kuroshio, the Pacific equivalent of the Atlantic's Gulf Stream. This brings tropical waters up past the east of the islands.

Japan is a very old civilisation, steeped in history, and it has long been associated with gardens, flowers and flower arranging, the latter the well-known Ikebana. Strictly speaking, Ikebana is the arranging of living plant material, but the name has come to be used to describe the art of Japanese flower arranging. There are many differing styles, but all share characteristic qualities – a concentration on line rather than mass, on simplicity rather than abundance. With the three main lines of Ikebana – *Shin* (heaven), *Soe* (man) and *Hikae* or *Tai* (earth) – the arrangers aim for a perfect harmony, beauty and balance, a wonderful thing to achieve in any form of artistic expression, I think. There are Ikebana societies all over the world now, on all the continents, and in the smallest countries such as Cyprus. There is probably no young lady in Japan who does not know how to do Ikebana – it's apparently one of the conditions of making a good marriage. New styles of flower arranging are now being introduced to Japan – I know of several Western-style arrangers, not me sadly, who have visited. Whether the Japanese take to it or not is yet to be seen. Our flower-arranging traditions are very new in comparison.

I don't demonstrate or teach Ikebana, as I haven't been taught the art, but I do admire many of the ideas, and adapt them for my own use. I'm very keen on many of the Ikebana containers made from native thick bamboo, one of which I've used for my Japanese arrangement. Traditionally cut into various shapes, they have different names: these include *Karimon*, wild goose gate, *Hoborizaru*, climbing monkey, and the one I used, *Sanjyu*, trifold. I've actually made something similar myself, with 4-5 inch (10-13 cm) bamboo from Kenya. I cut it into three lengths, 3, 3½ and 4 feet (90, 105 and 120 cm) and bound them into a triangular grouping with some thick raffia so they would stand well. I cut mouthpieces at various angles where I needed flowers, and wedged in little plastic pots to take floral foam. I use these containers because bamboo tends to split if it becomes waterlogged. This I know from bitter experience. In my youth, I sat a nice little bamboo container on top of the TV with some branches and flowers, and it exploded one night, splashing water down the back of the set and up the newly decorated walls. I won't repeat what my mother said! (Another water-reducing trick would be to coat the insides of the bamboo with polyurethane lacquer.)

Japanese gardens are some of the most beautiful in the world, I think, many of which are formal and containing water, rock formations, raked areas and miniature trees. Many of these latter are just small forms but some are the result of another Japanese art, bonsai. To the Japanese the garden is almost like a stage, the plant actors doing the bidding of the gardener-director, and nowhere is this more true than in the pines, junipers, maples, cedars and prunus which have been persuaded to remain small but look old.

Many trees and plants are indelibly associated with Japan. Pines are everywhere, in a sense the 'soul' of the Japanese landscape; they are symbols of strength and long life, and the main material in Ikebana. Along with the pines, maple trees, especially the dwarf varieties, are a major element of Japanese gardening with their two principal seasons, bright green in the spring and vibrant red in the autumn. The flowering cherries of Japan are perhaps the most famous trees, though, and thousands flock from the cities to see the spring displays near Kyoto.

Many flowers, too, principally the hydrangea and the chrysanthemum, are Japanese in origin and association. Carl Peter Thunberg (1743-1828), a Swedish doctor working at the Dutch trading post near Nagasaki, was the first to make the hydrangea known to Europe. The chrysanthemum, although bred in China and reaching Japan via Korea in AD 386, has acquired great importance in Japan. The flower has been the national emblem since the end of the eighth century, and the highest honour that could be bestowed on a citizen was the Order of the Chrysanthemum.

The Japanese undoubtedly have a special relationship with their plant materials, but in essence they are no different to flower arrangers anywhere else in the world – they share with us a love of Mother Nature's bounty. I hope very much one day that I can experience at first hand the wonders of that beautiful country.

Although Japan is most famous for the distinctive style of flower arrangement called Ikebana, my interpretation here could more justly be called 'oriental'. To emphasise this I've used a slatted bamboo screen as the background and as the base; the arrangement is done into a traditional double-decker bamboo container; and I've given the whole thing more height by placing it on a small bamboo table. Inside the bamboo container are deep metal dishes at the two levels to take the soaked floral foam for the two parts of the arrangement. The container stands about 3 feet (90 cm) high, and the finished arrangement is about 5 feet (1.5 metres). One of the principal beauties of traditional Ikebana arrangements is the simplicity, and this I think I've achieved here, creating something that almost looks as though it's sitting in a tranquil Japanese garden.

The outline material is acer or maple, a tree much loved by the Japanese and often used in bonsai. The leaves of *Acer palmatum* *'Atropurpureum'* are particularly ornamental, and the lovely bronze-red sprays sweep out to the left in the top arrangement, and to the right from the foot arrangement to create the outline height and width. It was a matter then of choosing a flower which was in keeping with the theme and the feeling of the arrangement. As I have a tremendous love of lilies – as

indeed do the Japanese; they are, I should think, third in popularity after chrysanthemums and carnations – I chose a magnificent 'Stargazer' lily as the focal point of both parts of the arrangement. These are arranged a little more 'tightly' in the top (because it's smaller in scale and proportion), more 'loosely' at the foot.

To bring the whole thing together, to create some depth, and to hide the mechanics, I have used the lovely round 'elephant's ear' leaves of the bergenia. This maroon foliage beautifully brings out the colour of the centre vein of the lilies and blends with that of the acer as well.

One of the most useful things about this sort of arrangement and container is that it can be used, of course, at all seasons of the year. The acer foliage, for instance, if picked at the right time, can last extremely well. Thus, if the flowers start 'going over' first, you can take them out, and replace them with fresh and new flowers – or indeed something quite different. That outline could outlast two or three different lots of flowers! Whatever type of home you have, I'm sure there is a position somewhere for this type of oriental arrangement.

An oriental arrangement to represent Japan, which has a feel of the art of Ikebana, and uses many materials which are traditional, such as the bamboo.

This is another arrangement which I think is very Japanese in feel, echoing the stark beauty of some of the best Ikebana, and the tranquillity of many a Japanese formal garden. The very simplicity of each stage should demonstrate how effortless such arrangements can be.

1 Placed on a wooden Japanese scroll base is a beautiful hand-thrown pottery container. This has sweeps and swirls of blue and green slip, giving a lovely sort of water movement. A branch of dried Kenyan thorn tree – I know it's not Japanese, but it creates the effect I wanted – is held by a large metal pinholder (because it is heavy, and must be supported properly). To hide the pinholder, I've placed large rough chunks of clear glass in the container.

2 To create a fresh foliage line, I've swept a branch of a variegated rhododendron – R. ponticum 'Variegatum' – to the front right.

3 Oriental arrangements must not be too cluttered so, as we started with such lovely voids, I've simply added two stems of 'longiflorum' lilies.

4 To bring in further shape and colour, I've added two sprays of leaves of helleborus (corsicus).

5 Behind the arrangement, now in all its finished glory, I've hung a colour-washed Japanese painting.

KOREA

Korea is a peninsular country in East Asia, lying between the Sea of Japan and the Yellow Sea. To the south and west of the peninsula are very many small islands. It is bordered to the north by China, with a tiny overlap with Russia. A country with a long history, it was occupied by Japan at the beginning of this century, and then partitioned after the war in the 1950s. The peninsula is now divided into South Korea (the Republic of Korea) and North Korea (the Democratic People's Republic of Korea).

Plains in the west rise to mountains in the north and east, which cover most of the country. The climate is much the same as most of Japan, maritime temperate, but because there is such a long north-south stretch, this can vary considerably. The mean temperature throughout the four seasons ranges from 41-57°F (5-14°C), and there is good rainfall. However, a naval officer on *HMS Belfast* in the Yellow Sea during the war in the 1950s, recalls winter 'pancake' ice in the north. The hottest month of the year is July.

In the north, the plants have elements in common with those growing in Manchuria. Trees include *Abies koreana*, the Korean fir, larches, thujas, pines, junipers, spruce and yew, as well as broad-leaved deciduous varieties such as *Quercus dentata*, the daimyo oak, birches, willows and syringas. There are varieties of ornamental rhubarb, and a member of the bilberry, cranberry, blueberry and whortleberry family, *Vaccinium ulginosum* which is regarded as a relic species, resulting from the climatic change which presumably occurred in the Tertiary Period. Many alpine plants are also found in the north.

In the central part of the peninsula and the western lowlands, vegetation of the temperate zone abounds: oak, hornbeam, birch, ash, shrub willow, lime or linden, forsythia (*F. ovata* is native to Korea), and several varieties of rhododendron. There is a grass which can be dried and used in flower arrangements, the *Miscanthus sinensis*, and chrysanthemums, balloon flowers (*Platycodon*), codonopsis, aconites and the Asian gentian.

In the warm south and the offshore islands, warm-temperate plants grow abundantly, many similar to those in the south-western part of Japan. There are camellia, privet, spotted laurel, euonymus, *Ficus pumila* (an ivy-like creeper we see as a pot plant), mandarin orange trees and elaeagnus (a shrub related to the myrtle and oleaster, and very good for foliage).

Other flowers of Korea include the bluish purple Rose of Sharon, *Hibiscus syriacus*, which is the national flower, the lotus, cosmos daisy, a bellflower, touch-me-not (*Impatiens roylei*, of the same family as busy lizzies), honeysuckle, iris, lilies of many varieties (*L. hansonii*, a martagon-type lily was found in Korea), peony, *Rosa rugosa*, hypericum, anemone and sedum.

The only time I've met Koreans was at the first WAFA conference in Bath in 1984. I had the great honour and pleasure of teaching some of the world delegates who included nine young ladies from Korea and a lady chaperone. They were accompanied by a male translator as well, for none of them could speak English. All the time I was speaking, he was interpreting, and they seemed to take it all in well, nodding and putting his (my) words into action. I did some of my Fabergé work with them, they never took their eyes off my hands, and they turned out some of the loveliest work I've ever seen from one of my classes. During the conference, I wandered around Bath to various demonstrations and receptions, and everywhere I went, there too were the nine young Korean ladies, who each time stopped, bowed, smiled, nodded – the pupils to the teacher. I'm sure all of Bath must have wondered what on earth was going on, and who on earth I was!

I don't know how many flower clubs there are in Korea, nor if they would welcome a visiting demonstrator at any time. If there ever were a chance of going, though, I'd be there like a shot!

To create the eastern feel here, to represent my feelings about Korea, I wanted to incorporate a magnificent bronze garden lamp which was a present from a club I visited in the Far East. These lamps come in all shapes and sizes; this one stands about 2½ feet (75 cm) high, and is a wonderful addition to my collection of flower-arranging accessories.

To give even more height to the grouping, though (it stands finally at about 4 feet/1.2 metres), I made a base for the lamp and the mechanics of the arrangement to stand on. This is a large piece of cardboard tubing – the centre of a roll of carpet, in fact – which I made into a solid column by cutting two discs of very thick card to fit top and bottom, and glueing very securely. I covered the whole thing with some paper which almost looks like leather, then spray-painted it in various brown and bronze colours, with a hint of gilt, to make a very appropriate lift.

The first placement as always, was the foliage to supply height and width. To create the rhythm and movement I wanted, I used the curly-wurly branches of contorted hazel (*Corylus avellana 'Contorta'*, Harry Lauder's walking stick). These, stripped bare as here, give a lovely delicate outline, very eastern I feel, and a little reminiscent of bonsai branches. These were lightly sprayed with gilt paint just to highlight them.

As outline to the sides further down in the grouping, I have used what I think is probably one of the most wonderful foliages - that of the camellia (a very eastern plant, the tea plant is a member of the camellia family!). This grows in a friend's garden and unfortunately doesn't flower (we know not why), but she lets me pick it, and it lasts for weeks. I've highlighted this slightly with leafshine just to give a little gloss: with the dullness of the texture and colour of both lamp and column lift, it could all have looked a little bland.

Once the outline was created on all sides, I chose soft pale pink and cream colourings, using a sweep of pink carnations to the left of the arrangement and, to the right, and coming up behind the lamp, a creamy pink-tinged lily. I grow this in my own garden – one of a big collection of about 30 types altogether – and it's called 'Chinook'.

The final touch, to add to the atmosphere of the grouping, was the lighting of the candle inside the lamp.

An atmospheric arrangement to represent Korea, utilising an eastern bronze lamp and fresh materials slightly reminiscent of bonsai.

Australasia

Australasia – the name coming from the Latin for 'to the south', or 'south wind' – is an imprecise term referring to lands in the Pacific Ocean, but which is more generally applied to Australia and New Zealand, and former dependencies such as Papua New Guinea.

There are several theories as to why the unique fauna and flora of Australia and New Zealand developed, chief among which is that of massive continental drift millions of years ago. Rather than evolving completely separately at first, the fauna and flora of Australia are thought once to have been part of larger genera when the land masses of Australia and New Zealand were 'attached' to the other continents, Africa and America. Several things hint at this one-time continental split. Sedimentary rocks in New Zealand indicate that the islands must at one time have formed part of a continental land mass, or certainly part of Australia. Continental coincidences occur too. In South America, Africa and Australia, there are natural habitats that resemble one another (the pampas, savannah and dry hinterland of Australia respectively): in these habitats, similar flightless birds exist, the South American rhea, the African ostrich and the Australian emu (and cassowary). New Zealand, too, has its unique flightless birds – the now extinct moa, killed off for food by the early Maoris (just as was the dodo in Mauritius), and the kiwi, the national emblem of the islands. The existence of *Nothofagus*, southern beeches, in both Australasia and South America is also said to suggest that land masses once joined have moved apart. Similarly, the banksia flowers unique to Australia, and the protea, as nearly unique to South Africa, are very alike, as well as both being members of the same botanical family.

Once the land masses had separated, however, the differences started to appear. It is the long oceanic *isolation*, so indispensably associated with the formation, development and success of species, that has led to the evolution of so many decidedly *odd* specimens, animal, avian and botanical, in Australia and New Zealand. If land links had existed recently (in geological terms), or if they had been nearer other continental masses from which seed-carrying birds could fly, or animals 'float', more highly evolved forms would have arrived and caused the extinction of older forms. The presence in both Australia and New Zealand of really quite primitive forms of animal life would seem to bear this theory out. There is a reptile in New Zealand, the tuatara, which is the only surviving member of an order of reptiles that lived some 200 million years ago and then died out except for this one species. A living fossil in fact.

And, of course, nowhere else except in Australia are there kangaroos and wallabies, nowhere else are there koala bears (who feed exclusively on the omnipresent eucalyptus trees, but only from about 20 of the 600 or so species). Nor does any other country or continent have anything like the duck-billed platypus, an oddity of a mammal that lays eggs, and has the beak of a duck, the body of an otter, and the tail of a beaver. Australia and New Zealand are quite unique, and I am privileged to have visited one, and to be about to visit the other.

AUSTRALIA

Australia, the smallest continent, lies in the Pacific Ocean, and includes the island of Tasmania to the south-east. The earliest inhabitants were the Aborigines, who came from south-east Asia. They had the country to themselves for some 20,000 years before the arrival of the European explorers, the Portuguese in the sixteenth century, then the Dutch. Captain Cook claimed the fertile east coast for Britain in 1770, and this area, known as New South Wales, was first used as a penal colony. (It's now a matter of pride in Australia to have criminal ancestors!) Australia celebrated 200 years since the founding of that first colony in 1988.

Australia is predominantly arid, becoming progressively drier towards the interior, which is hot desert. Small pockets around Perth in the extreme south-west and around Adelaide have a Mediterranean climate, and in Tasmania and around Melbourne, it is temperate. On the east are the eastern highlands, the Great Dividing Range, stretching north from Victoria through New South Wales up into Queensland, and these are partially covered by evergreen rain-forest. These zones make up only about 2 per cent of the continent's total area.

Australia is affected by two systems of rainfall, one to the south, from Antarctica, and one from the north which is monsoon. In the north-east you can find typical sub-tropical plants such as bromeliads, orchids and palms with, curiously, some conifers, trees normally associated with colder climes. In the open tropical woodlands around the rain-forest, are the eucalypts so typical of Australia, and acacia, with, after the rains, carpets of herbaceous flowers whose seeds might have remained dry and dormant for years. Further south, larger eucalypts are interspersed with the southern beeches also found in New Zealand. Casuarinas and acacias are the trees of the Mediterranean-type climates.

Many of the plants of Australia are as unique as its fauna, and the floral emblems chosen by each state reveal the diversity which has resulted from all the varied climatic conditions. Victoria in the south has a dainty plant, the pink heath (*Epacris impressa*); New South Wales has the waratah (*Telopea speciosissima*), a spectacular crimson flower. Queensland's emblem is the Cooktown orchid (*Dendrobium bigibbum*) which grows on trees as an epiphyte or on rocks as a lithophyte. The Northern Territories are represented by Sturt's desert rose (*Gossypium sturtianum*), a shrub whose flower is closely related to the hibiscus, and Western Australia by the kangaroo paw (*Anigosanthus manglesii*), a plant completely unique to Australia, with clustered woolly red and green flowers of about 3 inches (8 cm) long, which look a little like a kangaroo's foot. Sturt's desert pea (*Clianthus formosus*) is a trailing plant, one of those which blossoms in the dry region after rain, and is the emblem of South Australia. The blue gum (*Eucalyptus globulus*) is the emblem of Tasmania, and the golden wattle (*Acacia pycnantha*) in full bloom, with its yellow mimosa heads, is the national flower emblem of the whole of Australia, featuring on the coat of arms.

Australia was never on my list of places to visit, but when someone phones you up and asks whether you'd like to come over to demonstrate and teach, all expenses paid, you don't say no! I duly went with my wife, Pat, to Brisbane, Queensland. I had a great deal of help from the ladies of the flower club, who organised for me to pick in the Botanic Gardens. The director was a young man who had been at Kew and was amazingly knowledgeable. We went around in a little motorised vehicle, me picking, he collecting and putting them into the cool in the vehicle. The gardens needed re-establishing, and he had set up some areas with plants unique to or characteristic of various parts of the world - an African area, an Australian area and so on – and he was actually building up a little rain-forest. Although it was a lovely warm day, going through the trees with the stream, mosses and ferns, I did feel a little damp!

My first demonstration was for the gala evening to start the whole flower-arranging event off, and I was amazed at how far people had come. In the UK, 15 or 20 miles seems a long way, but many had flown 3,000 miles, and those from Northern Queensland had had a 36-hour train journey. These latter attended my workshops, bringing their containers and flowers with them: think of that 36-hour journey back with a *finished* arrangement!

I had a few days off, and on one was taken to a protea and leucospermum farm, on another a helicopter ride to the surfers' beaches. One afternoon I had free, I thought Pat and I might be able to pop up to what attracted us most in Australia – the Great Barrier Reef. On the map it didn't look too far, but the best place to view it from turned out to be Cairns, some 1,000 miles to the north! Some afternoon's trip that would have been, and just goes to show how vast Australia is. It was one of my major first impressions of Australia, and I hope very much that one day I can repeat the experience.

As my major impression of Australia was the sheer size and space of the country, I wanted to recreate that feeling in my arrangement. As it's also a country of enormous contrasts in climate, terrain and vegetation – because it *is* so big – that too I wished to represent. I was based in Brisbane, a wonderful semi-tropical area, but around Ayers Rock, in the centre of the continent, it is very barren and bleak. I think I've managed to capture those contrasts, the tropical feel and the space.

The piece of pine is in fact three pieces screwed together, and I immediately associated it in my mind with the emptiness of the hinterland of Australia. This sits on a base, a slice of wood which I sloshed with plaster to make it rough and earthy looking, then spray painted. The whole thing stands about 4½ feet (1.3 metres) high – you have to think big if depicting a large place, but the idea can, of course, be scaled down.

Slotted in to the right-hand side there are two curled palm fronds which I brought back from Australia in the green state – huge pleated shapes, almost like enormous table-tennis bats. As the edges browned, I clipped these off, until the fronds were reduced to almost half their size; then I left them to hang and dry completely when they twisted into these curls. They're lovely to use – creating a wonderful rhythm and very interesting textures.

To get the tropical effect, I used anthuriums which grow well in Australia (as they do in many other parts of the world). It was wonderful actually *picking* them there. These were slotted in at the foot of the arrangement into soaked floral foam in a container wedged into a very convenient cleft in the wood. At the top – to carry the line and the eye into the whole of the arrangement – I screwed a little metal tube into the back of the wood which took a cone shape of soaked floral foam and the two top lilies. Tucked in amongst the anthuriums are the wonderful shapes of dried banksias, which many people confuse with proteas. I brought these back from Australia fresh as well, and they dried very successfully, keeping their lovely bronzy-brown colouring. They're an excellent addition to this type of arrangement – or indeed any arrangement when fresh plant materials happen to be scarce.

Just to bring in a touch of green, I recessed at the top and bottom with the interestingly shaped variegated leaves of *Fatsia japonica*.

A minimum of detail, and striking shapes and colours which give, I think, a feeling of the tropics as well as the space and openness which, above all, Australia means to me.

A complete contrast in concept, giving a feel of massed lush tropical vegetation, the steamy swamps and rain-forest through which Crocodile Dundee might have stalked his prey.

1 *I always think it rather nice if on occasion you can make the container out of natural plant material. Here two pieces of hollowed palm stem (looking rather like the bottom part of a cycad) are bound with plaited raffia string at different heights, to tripod legs of dried water reeds. These tripods stand on a carved pine base, and yoghurt cartons in the palm stems hold the shaped wet floral foam.*

2 *Still keeping in touch with the natural plant material theme, the next placements are made-up bundles of eucalyptus bark: the twists, which naturally peel off the tree, were wired together, the wires twisted into a stem and anchored in the foam. These I have used in a diagonal line cutting across the very vertical lines of the reeds. For further interest, and to take away any squareness from the base, I added some pieces of dried fungus.*

3 *Unfussy flowers are needed for the fresh plant material in an arrangement like this. (Unfussy, because they have to do all the work on their own: an anthurium or any other flower that speaks for itself, could have been used as well.) As cymbidium orchids were available – they look so exotic and tropical – I thought they were just right.*

4 *To complete the arrangement, bringing it all together and hiding the mechanics, I used croton leaves. These plants grow in the wild in many parts of the world, and are readily available as house plants, in many colours and leaf sizes. Also occasionally known as 'Jacob's coat of many colours', their variegated reddy-bronze colours echo those on the lips of the orchids.*

5 *In all its glory, the arrangement – which stands about 5 feet (1.5 metres) high – shows just what can be done with the sparsest of ingredients and crafty containers home-made from natural plant materials.*

NEW ZEALAND

Situated in the Pacific, to the south-east of the huge bulk of Australia, New Zealand consists of two main islands, North Island and South Island, together with some smaller ones, including Stewart Island. New Zealand was one of the last island paradises in the world to be settled and explored. The great navigators of Oceania, the ancestors of today's Melanesians, Micronesians and Polynesians, are thought to have settled in the two islands in about AD 750. Because of the halo of clouds, these early Maoris called the islands Aotearoa, the Land of the Long White Cloud. Europeans didn't reach the islands until 1642 when Abel Tasman, a Dutch explorer, landed on Tasmania, naming it Van Dieman's Land, and on New Zealand, naming it Staten Landt, later Nieuw Zeeland (I presume 'new sea land'). Captain Cook explored the coast in 1769, and by 1840 the Maoris ceded the country to Britain by the Treaty of Waitangi. New Zealand was made a Dominion in 1907 and became independent in 1931.

Both main islands, covering an area slightly greater than that of Great Britain, are largely mountainous. North Island is partially volcanic, with geysers and the other sulphurous vents and cracks in the world's surface characteristic of volcanic activity; these are particularly numerous in the central plateau from Lake Taupo to Rotorua, the latter in the centre of Whakarewarewa Thermal Reserve, with roaring geysers, and constantly boiling mud pools. This vulcanicity is caused by New Zealand lying directly on what is called the Pacific 'ring of fire' (as do the Japanese islands), at the boundary of some of the earth's tectonic plates. On South Island, where there are no active volcanoes, a long chain of mountains, the Southern Alps, run down the length, deeply indented by fjords and lakes, evidence of past and indeed present glaciers.

The climate of New Zealand is temperate and mild, warm in the north, slightly cooler in the south. The mountains, which attract clouds crossing the Pacific, make for abundant rainfall and luxuriant plant growth. The north was once heavily forested, with such trees as the New Zealand kauri (*Agathis australis*), a stately conifer which yields oil and turpentine. In the south there are extensive forests of *Nothofagus*, the beeches of the southern hemisphere: the black beech, *N. solandri*, grows in the foothills of the Southern Alps, extending right up to the snowline. Above the forest levels, there are broad stretches of sub-alpine vegetation, with flourishing herbaceous plants: in the high alpine areas of South Island, the plant cover is mainly dwarf forms, grasses and mosses.

Many plants were discovered in New Zealand, and are unique to the islands. These include griselinia, a few species of fuchsia (discovered in 1834), *Ranunculus lyallii*, a buttercup, raoulia, a perennial ground-cover foliage plant, senecios and some cordylines. Perhaps the most distinctive indigenous New Zealand plant – and certainly one that is very relevant to we flower arrangers – is the New Zealand flax or hemp, *Phormium tenax*. This was discovered just over 200 years ago during Cook's first voyage, and still covers large areas of swamp land, especially in the south of North Island. The Maoris had used it extensively for making clothes and cord, and it is still used today as the fibres have a very high breaking strain. Sir Joseph Banks said that it was 'of a strength so superior to hemp . . . shining almost as silk and surprisingly strong'.

Other plants which I've only *heard* about, and haven't been able to identify or use yet, are *rewa rewa*, known as knight's excelsior, and the *ponga*. The existence of these has been revealed to me by the flower arrangers in New Zealand who have sent material in advance of my forthcoming visit in April 1990. It will be my first trip there – to Auckland, North Island, for a big flower convention – and I'm looking forward

to it enormously. 1990 is the 150th anniversary of the signing of the Treaty of Waitangi, and there are going to be many celebrations, highlighted by the January Commonwealth Games and a visit from the Queen.

I've often met New Zealand flower arrangers although I haven't visited their country yet, and they seem to be very enthusiastic. The Floral Arts Society of New Zealand has 116 affiliated groups, which means over 4,000 members! This all started in about the mid 1960s, and I've always noticed whenever meeting 'Kiwi' associates, that they have a great love for natural plant material. They use this *ponga* plant a lot in arrangements: it looks like pieces of dried wood, with fronds which, when dried, have wonderful curl and rhythm, looking rather like curled-up miniature ferns before they develop into the full leaf. They use a lot of New Zealand flax obviously, aspidistra and palm leaves, the blue gum, the vine of the kiwi fruit – again virtually unique to New Zealand, I'm looking forward to encountering that as foliage – and a profusion of flowers including gerberas, lilies, roses, carnations, helichrysums and freesias.

Everyone says New Zealand is like a Britain on the other side of the world, so I'm expecting lots of green, fresh and rolling countryside, and familiar as well as unfamiliar plant materials with which to work.

As New Zealand is a 'younger' country than Australia – it only became a British colony 150 years ago to Australia's 200 – it suggests modernity to me in flower-arranging terms.

On a base of a slice of wood, I arranged two modern hand-thrown containers. The top ewer I placed on a stand to give height, and the bottom pottery bowl – which has wonderful whirls overlaid on the slip and reminded me of the craters and mud pools of Rotorua – I wedged against the stand. A small container with soaked floral foam was fixed at the back of the taller of the two containers; a smaller one was hidden behind the bowl.

Although the shape of both pottery containers created a certain amount of rhythm and movement, they did look fairly static, so I needed something around them. I chose to use stripped pieces of contorted willow (*Salix matsudana 'Tortuosa'*), which were placed into the top foam-filled container, and swept to top left and bottom right. One smaller piece sweeps across the bowl, softening that uncompromising shape, from the bottom foam-filled container.

To bring fresh plant material into the arrangement, I used the stately stems of a tall peach gladioli as spine height: these also flow through the contortions of the willow to the right, giving a nice linkage with the trio of coral gerberas and the *Begonia rex*

foliage at the foot. The begonia variegations nicely pick up the colours of the two pottery containers.

To create the starburst effect in the top of the arrangement, I used two guzmanias, a house plant which is a member of the bromeliad family. It may sound like sacrilege to cut them off at the roots, but they last very well as cut plant material. (I did this because I didn't want to have to disguise a root ball.) I put each plant into a plastic test tube full of water and taped this to a thin garden cane to push into the foam.

The final foliage placements were the wonderful bronze-coloured variegations of the croton leaves to the left and, to the right of the guzmania, some leaves from another house plant, the spathiphyllum ('Mauna Loa' bears those tall arum-shaped flower heads).

The maroony-red throats of the gladioli pick up the red centres of the guzmanias and the croton and *Begonia rex* leaves, creating a flowing linkage throughout the whole modern-feeling and lively arrangement.

A modern arrangement for New Zealand, the swirls in the slip and the sinuous branches suggesting the hot pools, geysers and volcanic activity of North Island.

Europe

Although Europe spans so many countries and different cultures, and seems so large, it is the second smallest continent after Australia. It possesses below 10 per cent of the globe's land, but with about 15 per cent of the world's population, it is the second most populous continent after Asia. Europe stretches from Iceland and the topmost tip of Norway in the north to Malta in the south; from Portugal and western Ireland in the west to the Caspian Sea and the Ural Mountains in the east, the latter dividing European Russia from Asian Russia.

Europe in fact is a peninsula of the land mass of Asia, itself indented with peninsulas (Scandinavia and Italy) and offshore islands (the British Isles, Iceland, etc). Roughly it consists of a central plain extending from the Urals to the Atlantic, rising in the south to a series of mountain ranges – the Pyrenees, the Alps, Apennines, the Carpathians and the Caucasus –

and in the north to the mountains which are the spine of Norway and Sweden.

Climatically, Europe is dominated by three influences, the Atlantic Ocean, the cold land mass of Asia, and the hot Sahara in Africa to the south. The Atlantic waters much of the western parts of Europe and also feeds the virtually tideless Mediterranean. The Atlantic brings the Gulf Stream and North Atlantic Drift up as far as Norway and Iceland, so that in northern Europe zones of vegetation hardiness tend to stretch from west to east rather than from south to north. This contributes to one of the four main climatic zones of Europe, the temperate mild winters, cool summers and all-year rain of the north-west. More separated from the warmth of the Atlantic, the countries in central Europe tend to be influenced by the cold from the north and east, which makes for cold winters, warm summers and rain chiefly in summer. In eastern Europe and the north, there is the same belt of *taiga* that stretches across northern Canada, making for long cold winters, brief warm summers and very little rainfall. The Sahara warms up parts of southern Europe, particularly around the Mediterranean, to the same temperatures as in Florida, although that sub-tropical tongue of North America is on a latitude just short of 1,000 miles further south.

Belgium, France, Britain, Holland, both parts of Ireland, Italy, Malta and Switzerland are the European countries belonging to WAFA. But there are many other countries which are enthusiastic about gardens, trees, flowers, foliage and flower arranging. I've not been to Scandinavia, for instance, but I know that in flower-arranging terms, they do some wonderfully natural things at Christmas, with ribbon bows and the cones from the coniferous trees that cover so much of the individual countries. I've been many times to Germany to demonstrate, mainly to British Forces' wives who have formed groups now affiliated to NAFAS. (The base at Rheindahlen, one of my venues, is so big that it is international, with Americans, Canadians, Australians, French, you name it, and the club is virtually a WAFA all on its own!) A German woman, Franziska Bruch, was as much a pioneer in the new art of flower arranging as was Constance

Spry in England. Spain, too, which I visit a lot to rest and recuperate, has its flower-arranging societies, those with which I'm most familiar are on the coasts of the Costa Blanca and del Sol, and started by expatriates. Greece has some of the most beautiful wild flowers in the world, and I'm sure there must be some flower arrangers there.

Even the very smallest countries have this love: Luxembourg is known as 'le pays des roses'; and Monaco's tragically missed Princess Grace instituted a flower show held every year, and was greatly loved by flower arrangers all over the world.

Europe may not be the biggest of continents but it has had an enormous, even disproportionate, influence on the whole of world history. It was explorers from Europe who discovered the New World, it was botanists and travellers from Europe who found plants in every part of the globe, and Europe was responsible initially for the setting up of WAFA. Our languages may differ more than in any other continent, but we can all communicate easily through our shared language of flowers.

BELGIUM

Belgium is a country in north-west Europe, bordered by Holland and the German Federal Republic in the north and east, by the Grand Duchy of Luxembourg in the south, and by France to the west. The country is generally low-lying like its neighbour, Holland, and its main rivers, the Scheldt, the Meuse and others, are linked by canals which form an extensive system of inland waterways. The country is culturally divided, one proportion of the population in Flanders to the north speaking a dialect of Dutch or Flemish, the remainder in the south, the Walloons, speaking French. The floral emblem of the country, appropriately because of the associations of war with Flanders, is the poppy.

The Belgians are passionate gardeners, whether they have an actual garden, a balcony or even just a windowbox. Apparently the Belgians spend less on cut flowers than other Europeans, but more on house plants than any of us. In fact the main impression I got was that the Belgians seem to use house plants on their windowsills rather than draw the curtains! Favourites are sansevierias (mother-in-law's tongue to us, but lawyer's tongue in Belgium), ficus, monstera, ivies and ferns.

This interest in house plants is not just limited to individual homes, but Belgium herself is virtually a garden for house plants. There are hundreds upon hundreds of acres in the country given over to greenhouses which produce house plants for the rest of Europe. These flower- and plant-producing areas are chiefly in the north, around Ghent. Belgium produces most of Europe's pot azaleas, the majority of them available at Christmas. Begonias too are a major part of the 'industry', and millions flock each year to see the begonia fields in bloom.

There is a cut-flower industry in the area too, roses, carnations and orchids being particularly featured. And Belgium's flower shows are also world famous. The Ghent Floralies are held every five years at the Parc de la Citadelle, and the Floralia Palace was built for the 1950 show.

It's a few years now since I first visited Belgium, when I demonstrated in Ostend and Bruges. I am fascinated by markets of all types, and in the centre of Ostend there was a huge one, with stall upon stall of beautiful flowers – delphiniums, roses and what we don't see too much of in this country, natural bunches ready to put into an arrangement, things like sweetpeas and cornflowers, or sweetpeas and African violets, even cyclamens with geraniums. My venue in Ostend was a sort of schoolroom, rather cramped, but thankfully I was working smaller arrangements then. I was very pleased that so many spoke English because it could have been difficult, me not speaking very much French. However, of course, the language of flowers always has the upper hand, and it all went very well.

From Ostend, I travelled on to Bruges and I was going to demonstrate in the central square, in the lecture theatre of the bank. Needless to say, I arrived at rush hour (wherever you go in the world, there's always a rush hour), and to try and hop between about six lanes of traffic with my buckets of flowers, bits of driftwood, containers and what have you was rather hazardous. I had a couple of ladies helping me who were not quite so fleet of foot as I was, but we managed. The theatre was very plush, the demonstration went well, and once again, as in many places, I was pleased that so many men were in the audience.

My next trip to Belgium was in fact for the second WAFA conference in 1987, Belgium being one of the founder members of WAFA. The organisation at the venue, the Jardin du Botanique in Brussels, was superb. As soon as my car arrived, a steward spoke to me in immaculate English, had my car emptied of all my equipment, and I was taken to my position. An

envelope with instructions was given to me, and ground sheet, binliner and as much coffee as I wanted were provided. With invitations to lunch, to have a drink or a sandwich, and a virtually constant supply of Belgian chocolates, I've rarely been so well looked after in my life!

We were all allowed to enter only one class – fair enough as there were so many people from all over the world – and the one I had chosen was 'Foliage of the World'. I set up my container, an interesting log on which I could arrange three levels, and used foliages from the Caribbean, the Americas, Europe and Australasia. We had to disappear just after lunch while the judging went on, then return for the evening-dress preview when Queen Fabiola was to open the show. There were a lot of us competitors but she spoke to each one of us, shook our hands, told us how delighted she was to see us in her country, and made comments on the arrangements. This royal patronage was not only appreciated by all the Belgian flower-arranging societies but by everyone from around the world who had come to represent their countries. I also learned that I had won a silver, a particular delight with so much international competition. I shall never forget that visit to Belgium.

As the Belgians excel in growing house plants, I thought I would celebrate this aspect in a *pot et fleur*. This is always a class in flower competitions, and the rules read thus: 'An exhibit of growing plants which may or may not be flowering, in or out of pots, together with added fresh cut flowers. Accessories such as moss or driftwood may be included. It must be assembled in one container, and no added cut foliage other than that attached to the stems of the flower is permitted.'

A *pot et fleur* can either be small scale – a couple of plants with a flower or two in a bowl – or on the grand scale as here, about 4½ feet (1.4 metres). The container I used is in fact a garden birdbath, made of concrete which was 'antiqued' by spray-painting and then allowing the elements to add weathering, algae and so on. (I've talked about this in great detail in my last book, *The Crafty Flower Arranger*.)

I filled the birdbath with peat – I always use this as it retains moisture well – and took all the plants out of their pots, keeping the root balls intact. Flowing down to the right and across to the left I placed purple flowering bougainvilleas which create that nice line. To the right there is a lovely azalea, *the* plant I associate with Belgium. The centre of the arrangement is created with a magnificent *Begonia rex* in purple, grey and bronze colourings to link up with the bronzy look of the container.

Popping out underneath, to hide the peat, is a lovely little pink-spotted plant called hypoestes.

Giving more height to the arrangement, there is a purple and green leaved dracaena (one of these, *D. sanderiana*, is also known as Belgian evergreen), with, to the right-hand side, the wonderful flame-coloured rosette of the guzmania. This is a plant whose leaves overlap to form a water-retaining vase, a glorious 'flower' that isn't (the actual flowers are tiny and tucked in the brightly coloured bracts). The star-shaped plant which softens the area to the right is cordyline (often confused with dracaenas, and more commonly known as cabbage palm): this is a good house plant reaching 2-3 feet (60-90 cm) sometimes.

These pot plants look very attractive as a grouping in themselves, but to be a true *pot et fleur*, some fresh flowers are needed. I put some 'Stargazer' lilies into a water-filled plastic cone covered with coconut fibre (to blend in with the natural plant material), and inserted it at the back of the arrangement. To keep the flowers going, top the cone up with water, but when they do 'go over', change them for something else if you like – carnations next perhaps?

Belgium is world famous for her cultivation of house plants, and thus I have chosen to represent the country with a pot et fleur, *utilising many pot plants and some fresh cut flowers.*

As Belgium has always had such a love of gardening, I used some accessories to capture the olde-worlde charm of that long gardening tradition.

1 On a large wicker disc, I arranged an antique gathering trug, a treasured possession of mine, and a lovely big straw gardening hat (much more effective, I think, as an accessory). The containers to take the soaked floral foam for both parts of the arrangement were placed in the trug and in the bowl of the hat. In the trug the foam was taped into position for security; in the hat it was pushed on to a pinholder for extra weight, as I didn't want any water to spill out and spoil the soft material of the hat. I laid some sprays of corn in the trug to add initial interest.

2 The height of the trug arrangement was created with golden privet, and some wonderful golden ulmus or elm, a foliage which stays lime green through the summer months and is absolutely delightful to use. Flowing to the right-hand side, from the hat, the width is created by lovely sprays of stephanandra and golden privet, with Rosa rugosa in the middle.

3 Having created the basic outline, I now wanted to increase the foliage. To add a definite green and gold effect to the grouping, I've used some honeysuckle, Lonicera nitida 'Baggesen's Gold', some canariensis ivy and the deep

green of the wineberry. Coming back to the centre, to add depth, I used variegated weigela, and the lovely bronze tips of euphorbia.

4 Once these outlines were to my satisfaction, I followed the same lines with my flowers. The height was created with solidago or goldenrod, cream spray carnations flowing out either side, and spray chrysanthemums in a very soft, offbeat cream-to-peach colouring. I worked both arrangements at

the same time, the lower one flowing to the right, looking as if it were pouring out of the hat.

5 The main flowers in the centre are 'Mont Blanc' lilies, a lovely creamy beige picking up the colour of the hat, with a few little single spray chrysanthemums tucked into the centre to add a bit of weight higher in the arrangements. A good combination of colours and flowers.

FRANCE

France is a country in western Europe, bordered by Belgium and Luxembourg to the north-east, by the German Federal Republic, Switzerland and Italy to the east, and by Spain to the south. France was the Gaul that Caesar conquered in the first century BC, and the name comes from a Germanic tribe, the Franks, one of several groups of barbarians (the Goths and Vandals were others) which overran the country from the third to the fifth century. It was in the tenth century that Vikings or North Men established themselves in northern France, in what became Normandy, and it was these Nordic Frenchmen who later invaded England in 1066. There have been many wars in the history of France, the most famous perhaps being when the monarchy was overthrown in 1789. France is a republic, Europe's oldest state and largest country (excluding the USSR).

France has three seaboards, the English Channel (or La Manche) to the north, the Atlantic Ocean to the west, and the Mediterranean to the south. For this reason, the country enjoys three of the European climates, maritime, continental and Mediterranean. The soil is the main resource of France, 90 per cent of the land being productive. Fertile lowlands cover most of the north and west, rising to the Vosges, Jura and Alps in the east, the volcanic plateau, the Massif Central, in the south-east, and the Pyrenees in the south, on the border with Spain.

France is an agricultural nation, much of that fertile land given over to livestock and commercial cultivation of crops, ranging from cereals such as wheat and buckwheat to the specialities of various regions. In the north are grown things like potatoes, cabbage, artichokes, fruit and onions – think of those Breton onion-sellers, plaited strings of onions strung across their bicycles. In Normandy, similar to the Garden of Kent not too far away across the Channel, the main crop is apples for cider and Calvados. In the west, in the valley of the Loire, are grown mushrooms, hazelnuts, plums (for prunes), asparagus, shallots, and the harvest of the beech woods in the Périgord, the truffles. In the east, near the Alps, such things as walnuts and wild mushrooms are the specialities, with, a little to the west, Burgundy and its Dijon mustard fields and its blackcurrants for cassis. In the south, warmed by the Mediterranean climate, are the sun-loving herbs, the fragrant flowers grown for the perfume industry, all the ingredients for the best French ratatouille, olives and peaches.

Virtually throughout the whole of France, the vine is cultivated to produce grapes for the huge wine industry.

The French themselves are keen gardeners with a long tradition of *grand* gardens, such as those attached to the many châteaux. On a simpler scale, there are the *potagers*, or kitchen gardens. As befits a country so famed for its food, most of the French once devoted more of their land to food cultivation than they did to flowers and shrubs. This is now changing, and the French have also become very interested indeed in flower arranging; they are now a major force in the art. The French flower arrangers have the advantage of the different climatic zones in the country, and can choose between plant materials such as we might have in our gardens, and the more exotic materials available from the south, around Nice in particular, where palm trees line the seafronts of the plush coastal resorts. The wonderful *Routes Fleuries*, the long floral routes which characterise so many parts of France, have been instituted and planted by householders, local authorities and various organisations, and are also witness to the huge interest there is now in flowers there. Some of my major floral impressions of France include the windowboxes everywhere with their blazing red geraniums, and the open-air flower stalls in the markets, with their bunches of roses and violets – for the French are as known for *l'amour* as they are for their food!

Paris will be the host for the third WAFA show in 1990. Michel Cointat, Honorary President of WAFA and President of the Société Nationale d'Horticulture de France, says in his message to the association: 'With best wishes for success to WAFA, thanks to whom Paris will become the most beautiful flower arrangement in the world'.

As France is the gastronomic centre of the world, it seemed appropriate to represent the country with an arrangement composed almost entirely of fruit and vegetables – one of my favourite mediums in the art of flower arranging. The accessories too are culinary, the different woods and the texture of the basketry contrasting well with the wonderful shapes, colours and textures of the plant materials – for they *are* plants after all.

Because of the weight involved here, the first priority was to ensure that the mechanics of the arrangement were very firmly anchored. I used a large hessian-covered base, and the first placement was the large gathering basket to the left. The dark wooden barrel end at the back (Bacchus grinning away) was supported on a metal rod, again with a very heavy base, which gave both stability and held some of the elements of the arrangement together. The lower basket to the right-hand side was then wired to the original basket, followed by those at the top.

As with a flower arrangement, it is the height that must be created first, to get the edge of your 'frame', and this I created with a string of garlic, that flavouring so olfactorily associated with France. The sheaves of corn and the sweetcorn create width as well as height, with the spring onion stalk clusters looking like a firework burst. The wooden rolling pins towards the base created another

angle with, above them, a space that needed to be filled with something visually large. This did not necessarily have to be colourful, so I chose a magnificent Savoy cabbage, and placed its cut stem in a container of soaked floral foam to keep it fresh.

The right-hand sweep of the arrangement is created by the French bread sticks, a pottery bottle such as might hold an old brandy, and various wooden spoons and spatulas. As a magnificent centrepiece, I used the cut watermelon, the pink and black adding singing colour to the grouping. The green cauliflower placement started to bring the arrangement in towards the middle, with some yellow peppers, magnificent mushrooms, nutty brown bread, broccoli and red peppers. At this stage, the main general flow through the centre of the arrangement had been established, so filling in was needed. I used various other little additions of fruit and vegetables – tomatoes, grapes, a turnip, some leeks and those sprays of crabapples.

All the ingredients for the arrangement were mounted on wooden skewers or saté sticks. *Never* use metal, as the fruit or vegetable will quickly go rotten and you can't then use the ingredients afterwards.

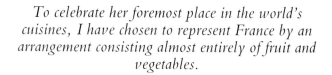

To celebrate her foremost place in the world's cuisines, I have chosen to represent France by an arrangement consisting almost entirely of fruit and vegetables.

GREAT BRITAIN

Great Britain is the largest island in the British Isles and in Europe, and it consists of Scotland, Wales and England plus various very much smaller islands around the coastline, ranging from the Shetlands in the extreme north of Scotland to the Isles of Scilly (or the Scillies) in the extreme south-west of England. Other islands are often not, strictly speaking, thought of as part of the United Kingdom (which consists of Great Britain plus Northern Ireland): the Isle of Man has been virtually self-governing for years, although a British Crown possession since 1828; and the Channel Islands, too, are dependencies of the British Crown. Both have their own legislatures and taxation systems.

Great Britain consists of lowlands and highlands, the Snowdonia range to the east in Wales, the peaks of the Pennines and the Lake District in the north of England, rising to the Grampian and Cairngorm Mountains in the north of Scotland where Ben Nevis is situated, the highest point in the island. Because of the long north-south stretch, the climate varies quite considerably, but generally it is maritime temperate. A major influence, of course, is the Gulf Stream which sweeps up the west side of the islands. If the Shetlanders have such short days that they cannot grow much (they probably knit instead), in the Scillies the temperature is so much milder that they can produce early spring flowers for the UK market, their main source of income apart from tourism.

Flower arranging in Great Britain is a fairly new art. The Edwardians and Victorians did, of course, appreciate flowers and house plants – think of the good old aspidistra – but I would say that it wasn't until the beginning of the 1930s that flower arranging proper took off. Most of the credit for this has to go to the late Constance Spry: a great free-stylist, she was a pioneer in an unexplored territory, making us all aware of the magnificent things Mother Nature produces for us. It was she who introduced sprays of berries and the use of fruit and vegetables to arrangements, the latter one of my own passions (whether this is due to the fact that she died on my birthday many years ago, I don't know).

Since then, of course, there have been many great exponents and teachers of the art, but it wasn't until 30 years ago that NAFAS – the National Association of Flower Arrangement Societies - came into existence. Only a few clubs joined at the beginning, but now almost every town and village in the UK has a flower club, and that small association has become, for want of a better expression, very big business. What started off as a small group of enthusiastic lady flower arrangers has now developed into a tremendous organisation. As a professional flower arranger, I have to travel the length and breadth of the country, demonstrating to these clubs, and I never cease to take pleasure in the fact that I can go to almost any corner of Britain and meet people on the same wavelength as myself, people who love plant material and who love arranging it.

I am particularly glad to be a flower arranger in Great Britain, because here we can enjoy four seasons. In more exotic climes they may have a rainy season, or a heatwave, but they can't ever enjoy the wealth of plant materials that the four distinct seasons of our temperate climate offer us. I know that clever growers around the world can now make available almost anything at any time of the year, but I still think the *seasonality* is what makes flower arranging in Britain so varied and so exciting (the day they bring daffodils out in the middle of July is the day I give up).

In spring, for instance, just the sight of the green buds on the trees, or the first glimmer of colour on forsythia, is a great joy to me. At this time, we have the wonderful bulb flowers - daffodils, narcissi, hyacinths and tulips – all wonderful for flower

arranging. In summer, of course, there is an over-abundance of every conceivable type of flower and foliage. That's when you can identify flower-arrangers' gardens. They're the ones that are almost entirely green (my own garden has been called a green oasis), growing the many varied and textured foliage plants that are difficult to buy – things like hostas and ivies, for instance, that no serious flower arranger can be without.

In the autumn, we have the magnificent colours, mists and mellow fruitfulness, and again a wonderful time for flower arrangers, with colour-changed foliages, berries, crabapples and seed pods, all of which can be used in flower arrangements. This is the time for drying and glycerining, for preserving plant materials for later use. In winter it is usually difficult to find fresh plant materials, but this is when – particularly at Christmas, *the* time for flower arrangers – you can make use of those preserved materials, gilding or spray-painting the bulrushes, cones, grasses or seed pods that you so carefully garnered and stored in the autumn.

Other countries in WAFA may *think* they have seasons, but none can ever be so richly varied as ours. I love *every* month of the year for the slightly different edge it gives to the arrangements I create and the ideas the materials inspire.

I think in this country we are very traditional in our outlook on flower arranging (despite forays into abstract, Ikebana and the new European style), which is why in this section the arrangements have been designed in a traditional mode. This one, with the combination of candles, wood and metal, is like a British still-life, looking as if it might be quite at home at a medieval banquet.

The accessories create the mood. The candelabra is spelter - a metal used by the Victorians as a cheaper alternative to bronze – and this stands on an oak stool which also takes the higher arrangement. The lower arrangement spills from an oak bible box, and I've also used the ornately carved front piece of another bible box as an accessory at the base of the arrangement, with pewter goblets and plates of various sizes. The containers for both arrangements are plastic, holding soaked floral foam held in place with floral foam tape.

The basic idea for the arrangement was to have the top higher than the candles – the plant materials must always predominate – and then to sweep down to the left, echoing the curve of the large pewter plate, then to curl around to the right. The height was created with a spine piece of *Rosa rubrifolia* – a wonderful foliage to have in your garden – which sprays to the sides as well. Other backing foliages here are sprays of grey helichrysum, a lovely ruby

form of acer or maple and, to bring the centre of the foliage part together, *Hosta sieboldiana* and bronze peony foliage. Both arrangements contain these – they must complement each other – and it is only when you are entirely satisfied with this 'backing' to your still-life that you start to place your flowers.

With these, you follow the same line created by the foliage, starting at the top with two or three flowers, then coming down towards the centre with smaller flowers, before filling in the actual centre – the heart of any traditional massed arrangement – with your most spectacular flowers. The height here was created by lovely 'Gerdo' roses in a wonderful offbeat peachy pink (a commercial rose which has recently became very popular), and some pink 'Sim' carnations. I recessed with some garden plants – lovely grey-pink hydrangeas, some sprays of clematis (these *do* condition well, despite what many people think), and some 'Autumn Joy' sedum. This gives a lovely depth to the arrangement before the principal flowers – the three types of lily – are positioned. These are 'Prominence' (pink), 'Mont Blanc' (cream) with, between them, the lovely pink trumpets of the *Amaryllis belladonna*, which I think is absolutely delightful.

A truly magnificent arrangement which, I think, sums up traditional British flower arranging at its best.

1 In a lovely cherub container made of moulded resin, and holding soaked floral foam, I started to establish the outline of the arrangement. This consists of the height and width. For the height I've used sprays of Rosa rubrifolia, *canariensis* ivy and *berberis,* the latter two also sweeping to the sides. This outline will act as a 'frame' for the remainder of the arrangement.

2 This step consists of thickening up the outline and starting to think about the centre of the group. I've used camellia foliage to add that darker centre to the arrangement, along with two hostas, 'Albo-marginata' and 'Albopicta'. I've also used larger leaves of the *canariensis* ivy and one or two bergenia leaves. The whole centre is now nice and full, giving the depth that will be needed when the rest of the plant material is placed in position.

3 At this stage the arrangement is still all foliage – and indeed I didn't want to use any flowers at all because it was an autumn arrangement and I had all the wonderful berries at my disposal. Following the same lines as the initial foliage placements, I used some golden privet to give a little lightness and variegation, and echo the hosta's yellow edges. The sprays of cotoneaster berries coming in from the sides link up with the sprays of crabapples.

4 As a final placement, I've put in the centre some wonderful clusters of rowan berries. Sprays of rowan are extremely heavy and can overbalance a container if you're not careful, so what I do is use the berry clusters only, wiring them and their stems together then pushing the metal leg into the floral foam.

This is a stylised, traditional pedestal-type arrangement, one which wonderfully illustrates the ways in which our seasonal materials can be used.

5 Just to pull the whole idea together, and to add extra interest, I've put an extra little group at the foot of the cherub container, using the ivy, rowan and crabapples.

HOLLAND

Holland, or more properly the Netherlands, is a country in north-west Europe, bordered by the Federal Republic of Germany to the east, Belgium to the south and the North Sea to the west and north. The Dutch were great explorers and colonists in the seventeenth century, and much botanical knowledge was gained at this time by their importation of plants from around the world, from Africa, America and China, etc. Europe owes the introduction of the pelargonium and chrysanthemum to them, for instance.

The whole of Holland is low-lying, as we know from the story of the boy who stuck his finger in a hole in a dyke. Much of it has been reclaimed from the sea, with some 40 per cent of the land below sea level. Rivers, including the Scheldt, Maas and Rhine, have been linked with the many famous canals to form a very efficient inland system of waterways. Because of this flatness and abundant water – the climate is much the same as that in the UK – Holland is a country given over very much to agriculture, and a large proportion of the vegetables available in the UK are grown there.

Holland, though, is as well-known as Belgium for its cultivation of flowers and foliages, in particular for tulips, the country's national floral emblem. These were introduced from Turkey and the Levant, called *tulipan* by the Turks. According to the writer Hakluyt, the first bulbs planted in England were sent from Vienna at about the end of the sixteenth century. But it was in Holland that tulip mania truly took hold: prices of the bulbs in the seventeenth century rose to above those of precious metals; estates were gambled and lost because of tulips; and single bulbs were exchanged for ludicrous sums, one in the 1650s for about £450, a vast fortune then. The enthusiasm continues, if not in so feverish a fashion, with over 30,000 acres given over to the bulbs – a sight to see in the spring, on the floral routes north of Leiden. Gladioli, narcissi, crocuses, hyacinths and iris are also grown in the bulb-fields. There are hundreds of nurseries throughout the country cultivating flowers for cutting, as well as shrubs and trees, and one commentator has quite justifiably called Holland the 'garden supplier to Europe'.

I first visited Holland not long after I'd completed my National Service. This was before I took up any form of flower arranging, and I'm sure my trip really did spur me on to spend my life with flowers. The Keukenhof Gardens at Lisse (*keukenhof* means kitchen garden) are spectacular; almost every season of the year it's a paradise for garden lovers and flower arrangers. Over six million bulbs bloom in the spring there, and they have glasshouses where bulbs are developed and more delicate varieties nurtured. I wandered around for hours.

I was also taken, on that first visit, to the Aalsmeer flower auction, the largest in the world. Although computerised now, it still works on much the same principle as then. My guide was the uncle of a friend, a florist in Amsterdam. He had a seat in what was almost like a theatre in the round, with tiers, and wanted to buy a great number of pink roses. As a trolley holding about 100 bunches was brought out, the auctioneer started off the bidding at the highest price, with an enormous clock on the wall also starting to move anti-clockwise. The further round the clock needle goes, the lower the price becomes, and it is a matter of knowing how much you need or want to pay, and getting in at the right time before anyone else. When you press a buzzer to stop the clock, you don't actually have to buy the complete contents of the trolley – you could take five or ten bunches, and the bidding would re-start. However, my companion bought the lot, much to the disgust of the other bidders.

After being bought, the flowers are delivered to the packing rooms,

and I have to give full credit to the Dutch for the magnificent way in which they pack their flowers. These are immediately loaded on to lorries and taken to a multitude of destinations, many to flights that will wing the flowers all over the world. Aalsmeer is an absolute must when visiting Holland, quite rightly known as the World Flower Centre.

The other abiding impressions of Holland are the flower stalls in open-air markets, the flowers arriving, leaving and being sold from the canal barges in Amsterdam and Rotterdam, and the wonderful *little* arrangements that you can buy. These are actually made up by the florist – something like a tiny pottery container with a miniature pinholder securing a little twist of wood and three gerberas as a complete arrangement. These are what you buy for your hostess when going for dinner instead of taking her a bunch of flowers which she will have to arrange herself. A lovely idea, and a lovely gesture.

Flower-arranging clubs in Holland proliferate, but they are very much smaller in size; sometimes only about sixteen people meeting once a month in someone's house. Still, they are as enthusiastic as the rest of us, and go in a lot for teaching, learning and developing styles (such as the one overleaf). Dutch flower arrangers are also very talented – one beat me to the gold in the last WAFA show in Brussels!

Holland is a country very much associated with its flower industry, probably one of its biggest. Anyone who has had the joy and pleasure of visiting the country will feel what I do, that it represents above all, flowers of every variety.

I think also that the Dutch flower arrangers were the prime movers in a new European style, in which the flowers seem to be clustered together in groups, visually looking very natural. It's a style that I can't say I'm over-enthusiastic about, but I do admit it can look very effective and does have its point. It's quite different to the flowing lines that British flower arrangers seem to aim for.

The containers I've used here are two dark blue ceramic dishes, one balanced on top of the other to give the two different levels. Long strips of soaked floral foam were wedged to the back of each container. The first placements were three groups of fine willow twigs in the top-level container which create the height. These made a good support for the groups of blue iris and the acacia with its yellow mimosa-like flowers: these gave the flower height in all three separate groupings.

To add another shape and to echo the yellow of the acacia and that streak on the petals of the irises, I added some sprays of 'Connecticut King' lilies, lower down and coming forward in the central group. To the right-hand side, I added a cascade of yellow 'Frisco' roses.

To hide the mechanics to the right-hand side, the wet floral foam, I used pieces of bun moss and some variegated leaves of the canariensis ivy. To the left-hand side, to hide the foam as well as to link the higher container with the lower, I used three pieces of dried brown fungus. This led to the fourth placement of flowers which spring from the soaked floral foam in the back of the bottom container, again several 'Frisco' roses, and some of the same yellow lilies. To hide the front of these, and also to bring in its wonderful rounded shape, I added a mound of the bun moss so that the visual weight was carried from one side of the arrangement to the other.

An interesting idea, and it would look very effective indeed in the right setting.

Holland is a country famous, above all, for its flower industry, and it has also been influential in creating new flower-arranging styles such as that shown here.

IRELAND

I shall talk about the two parts of Ireland together partly because I have not demonstrated in Northern Ireland (although I have visited and marvelled at the beauty of the countryside), and because, despite politics, they are not too different botanically or as far as the world of flower arranging is concerned.

The island of Ireland, the second largest in the British Isles, is separated from England, Scotland and Wales by the North Channel, the Irish Sea and St George's Channel. The island as a whole consists of a central lowland area of fertile plains, bogs and moorland, rising to hills and mountains in the south. The island is largely agricultural, and its famous rain and dampness – that which is supposed to make the skins of Irish maidens more fair – contribute to the green pastures which produce beef cattle, butter, cream, cheese and prize-winning racehorses. (That water also produces several forms of alcohol – wonderful whiskeys in both south and north, and several varieties of dark stout.)

Ireland not only enjoys the maritime climate of the rest of the British Isles, but it also benefits generously from the Gulf Stream. This is a warm current, one of the most powerful of the world's sea currents, which brings heat from Florida up towards the coasts of Europe. (The North Atlantic Drift, the northern extension of the Gulf Stream, takes the warmth further up to the coasts of Iceland and Norway.) Many gardens on both east and west of Ireland demonstrate how this warmth can change the botany. In Dublin, for instance, things seem to grow much bigger, better and fatter than they do in my Yorkshire garden. In Cork, in the garden of a very wonderful gardener and flower arranger, Maude Kelly, I saw my first Chilean fire tree, something I would never have believed could grow anywhere this side of the equator. In some of the magnificent gardens in Northern Ireland, the winters are so mild that plants grow there that do not grow anywhere else in Britain – Cape geraniums can winter outside, for instance. To clarify the effect of the Gulf Stream even further: most of Northern Ireland lies on approximately the same latitude as Moscow in the east and Labrador City, Canada, in the west. And in Inverewe, a spectacular garden even further north on the west coast of Scotland, also blessed by the Gulf Stream, palms, bamboo, eucalyptus and other sub-tropical plants flourish.

One of my trips to Eire, to demonstrate to the Horticultural

Society of Ireland, shows that not everything in the garden can be rosy for the flower-arranging demonstrator. I set off on the night ferry with my car below deck, and arrived on the morning of the demonstration in the evening. My car duly came off to go through Customs, but then they could see more in the back of my estate car than simply suitcases. Bits of driftwood under polythene sheeting, greenery and flowers in buckets, and pieces of metal (stands) must have looked a trifle suspicious, so I was confronted by a young Customs inspector. He obviously hadn't encountered a flower arranger before, and didn't know what I was on about. 'This lot can't, of course, come into the country,' he said. Trying to keep calm, I explained what I was doing, that I had demonstrated many times before in his country, and that I had never had this kind of trouble before. He said that no vegetation was allowed to move between Great Britain and Ireland, and that it all would have to be incinerated.

I stood my ground as I knew there were a lot of people coming to the dem that night, and that I couldn't possibly gather enough material in the time left. But he too stood his ground, each of us as adamant as the other, and I had to call upon the help of the HSI committee member with whom I had been dealing. The Customs man wouldn't even budge

then, and eventually we had to contact the Minister of Agriculture – a friend of a friend of a friend. He issued a docket saying that the plant material could be brought in for the demonstration, but had to be incinerated afterwards.

That didn't please me over-much, but at least the demonstration could go ahead. I enjoyed driving away from the Customs House, leaving a very disgruntled young official who had been confronted and thwarted by his very first flower arranger. The dem went well, and I did discover later that there was a chrysanthemum bug around at the time; my young opponent, not knowing a chrysanthemum from a gladiolus, had thought I was importing a carload of bugs!

I've driven a lot round Ireland, both north and south, and essentially it has a beautiful tranquil countryside. I've experienced the Irish friendliness – I meet up and catch up with many Irish friends at our national and international events – and I've experienced the overwhelming Irish hospitality. Afternoon tea in Ireland, I warn you, can be a killer, consisting as it does of all the usual tea and cakes, but also of mugfuls of whiskey! I've also taken note of the Irish drivers – they never seem to be driving in the direction in which they're looking! Apart from these few 'drawbacks', I have very loving memories of Ireland and look forward to returning.

For Eire, in southern Ireland, I wanted to create something green, for despite their differences, both parts of the island are a beautiful green. This is particularly true of the south because it is so affected by the Gulf Stream, and a few more lush and unusual green things can be found there.

As I wanted to create a fairly traditional arrangement, the china urn was an obvious choice. This held two blocks of soaked floral foam used upright because of the intended height of the arrangement, around 5 feet (1.5 metres). Because of that height, I was really able to go to town on materials, some from my own garden, some imported, and some gathered from friends and relatives.

For height and outline of the arrangement, I used moluccella, bells of Ireland (not, despite the name, native to the country). In the natural state these are a wonderful limey green, something much coveted by all flower arrangers, but the two pieces here had been bleached and glycerined. To give a dark line at the top, I also used some very tall flag iris foliage, wonderful for a backing. Sweeping down to the sides off to the right, there are two types of ivy: one used to be called 'Paddy's Pride', then became 'Sulphur Heart', and I believe this is going to be changed in turn (I'm sticking to the first name); the other is good old canariensis. On the left, the foliage is a must for every flower arranger's garden, the

griselinia.

After the three basic parts of the outline were established, it was a matter then of bringing in the next outlines, ferns of one sort or another. More central placements were then necessary and to the left I've got a wonderful variegated *Fatsia japonica* leaf which sits behind the variegated decorative kale. (These are very showy, and you can grow them easily in your garden, although they do prove their membership of the cabbage family after a few days in an arrangement!) To the right, there is a white-edged hosta and a variegated rhododendron (*R. ponticum* 'Variegata').

To bring the centre together, and link with the cream of the moluccella, I used double cream delphiniums which start high and sweep down to the left, and which are interspersed with the delicate creamy fronds of astilbe. In the centre, to give real weight, I've got some wonderful heads of artichokes. Other green additions are huge fronds of amaranthus (Dutch grown, about 3 feet/90cm in length), camellia foliage, and hydrangea heads. To echo the cream colourings of the delphiniums and moluccella, I've used pieces of a cream and white euonymus and some cream 'Mont Blanc' lilies.

A lush traditional array of the green for which southern Ireland is so famous, basking in the warmth brought northwards by the Gulf Stream.

As for Eire, the first thing that comes into my mind when I think of Northern Ireland in flower-arranging terms, is the greenness. It's not quite so lushly and exotically green as Eire perhaps, because it is further north, but the 'wearing of the green' is as true of Northern Ireland as of Eire.

The clean and fresh, newly minted and rain-washed feel of the northern counties could only be reproduced by a clear, fresh colour to match the green, and so I chose white flowers (pink, apricot or cream would have been completely wrong). Another impression is that of a *softness* in both parts of the island, due perhaps to the amount of water which provides all that green. It's very noticeable, even in the Irish voices.

For my green Northern Ireland arrangement, I chose a very large green acrylic tray as a base for the tall slender green glass bottle with stopper. Behind this was a flat dish holding the soaked floral foam into which the arrangement was built.

As the bottle is rather tall and powerful, the arrangement obviously has to be in proportion, so the height was created with tall iris leaves, and width with ferns and griselinia. People say this is too tender for Britain, but I've had a plain green one in my northern Pennine garden for over 15 years, and it's approximately 15 feet (4.5 metres) high. It does need the protection of a south-facing wall though, and I believe the variegated one is less hardy. I would not be without my griselinia because its foliage is the same throughout the whole twelve months of the year – whether you need sprays in July or January, you can still pick it.

To add weight to the centre of the arrangement I used plain green hosta leaves. Following the same lines as the outline material, white gladioli give height towards the back of the bottle. Swinging down to the left-hand side there are sprays of *longiflorum* lilies and white carnations. For recessed plant material I used white spray chrysanthemums and a white flowering hebe.

Extra placements, to soften the outline further, were of a cut flower which comes in from South Africa and lasts for weeks in water. This is the chincherinchee (*Ornithogalum thyrsoides*), which I've used here still very much in the green bud state, but which will eventually break out into its white flowers. (A close relation is *O. umbellatum*, the little white, lily-like flower known as star of Bethlehem, and which is hardy enough to be grown in Europe and southern England.)

Final foliage placements to 'green' up my arrangement are, to left and right, *Mahonia japonica* and *Helleborus corsicus*.

Another green arrangement, with crisp white flowers, to represent my reactions to Northern Ireland.

Ireland, north and south, is steeped in history, and everywhere you come across wonderful antique shops. All flower arrangers are, by nature, collectors of one sort or another, and I thought it would be interesting to show how individual collections could be used in tandem with flowers.

———————————

1 First of all I set up the basic 'frame' for my floral picture, arranging a Tunbridge Ware sewing box, some old leather-bound books, and a drinking horn on top of the box. This box is one of a pair, Germanic in origin I think, and purely decorative. I lined the interior with very thick polythene to prevent it being water-damaged. A wedge-shaped piece of soaked floral foam was then inserted, pointed end down.

2 To create the outline, I used a lovely ivy, 'Chicago', which is variegated and very delicate. This flows down to the left-hand side, softening the hard line of the horn, with some sprays, very much shorter, to the right. To give height, I used the lovely foliage of the helichrysum: this is also used as a focal point in the centre together with some canariensis ivy.

3 To start on the flower part of the arrangement, I used pale pink spray carnations. These give height and flow down to the left. The next placement was the lovely creamy pink alstroemeria, the Peruvian lily, in the higher right and flowing just past the centre to the left.

4 Now come the main flowers. One is the lovely 'Handel' rose, with a creamy base and pink lips: it comes from Holland and has a slight perfume. To give depth of colour and a different form, to the right and flowing down to the left are lovely dyed and dried scabious heads. The final flowers, tucked in, are lovely little bobble spray chrysanthemums.

5 To finalise the arrangement, I added the second horn, sweeping in the opposite direction to its partner. I also used the decorative top of the first horn as an accessory. There are good levels here, and the varied interests of the wood, leather, horn, silver and plant material, and it does show, I think, how you can use some of your collected bits in 'collection groupings' like this, along with your flowers.

ITALY

Italy is the peninsular country in southern Europe which looks like a high-heeled boot set within the Mediterranean, kicking the football which is Sicily. The Republic of Italy includes the island of Sardinia to the west of its 'ankle', across the Tyrrhenian Sea. Italy is bordered in the north by the Alps, and the countries of France, Switzerland, Austria and Yugoslavia; to the east her seaboard is on the Adriatic, to the south the Ionian. The spine of the country is formed by the Apennine Mountains, the only lowlands being narrow coastal plains and the valley of the Po River in the north.

The climate of Italy is varied, both because of its position and because of the two dominating elements of its landscape, the mountains and sea. The 'joint' with the rest of Europe is the massive range of the Alps and there typically alpine temperatures prevail, very cold in winter and gentler in summer. The lower portion of the Alps which slope gently to the Lombardo-Venetian plain, is characterised by a series of fjord-like lakes, hollowed out by long-disappeared glaciers. Here, around the three principal lakes, Maggiore, Lugano and Como (the first shared with and the second virtually enclosed by Switzerland), flowers more associated with Switzerland, such as gentians, periwinkles and cowslips, bloom in the spring.

The great valley of the River Po, which stretches from Venice in the east through to Piedmont and the Maritime Alp border with France in the west, is the prime agricultural area of Italy. Dairy cattle are reared, and butter is the cooking medium (in the warmer south, with few cows and an abundance of olive groves, olive oil is used). The well-irrigated land here is also where rice is grown for the Italian *risottos*; this is the major rice-producing area in Europe. Here too are grown the vines for the many varied wines of the country, including the Venetian *prosecco* and the famous Chianti.

The Alps to the north and the beginning of the Apennine 'spine' to the south create great temperature differences: Turin, for instance, can be colder in winter than can many cities in Scandinavia; the Italian Riviera, not too far to the south-west, is protected from Arctic winds by the Apennines, and enjoys the mild Mediterranean climate of the rest of Italy as far south as Naples. Here the climate becomes almost North African, with little rain and that only in winter, and some summer temperatures as high as those in Florida and the Caribbean. Apart from the typical grey-green of the olive groves, there are palms here, all the Mediterranean flowers, the vegetables that add the heat to southern Italian cooking, and the fruit-tree blossoms which perfume the air.

Italy has had a rich and extraordinary history. The country spawned the Roman Republic and Empire, whose colonising led, in botanical terms, to a huge spread of plants throughout Europe. The legions, for instance, would carry with them the seeds of plants they needed or could not live without, to cultivate in the countries they occupied; many herbal plants and fruits in England were introduced by the Romans, some actually growing mostly along the routes taken by the soldiers, seeds perhaps having fallen from toga pockets!

Ancient Rome was also responsible to a very large extent for the whole of European gardening. The *atrium* of Roman villas, the open courtyard in the middle, was where people strolled, sat in the sunshine, ate, and admired the plants – a garden in other words. These plants were grown in terracotta pots, jars and urns which even today make the best containers for outdoor and indoor plants, having been in use for at least 2,000 years (the plastic versions are a travesty in comparison). The Romans are thought to have grown flowers such as the violet, poppy, iris and lily,

as well as many herbs, fruit and vegetables. They also grew roses, often in 'greenhouses' heated by steam (no trouble to people who introduced steam baths and under-floor heating to their villas in chilly England).

Some Roman gardens were created which extended beyond the *atrium* but few of these are extant today. There are, however, very many beautiful gardens throughout Italy, many dating from the time of the great city states and their sumptuous courts, and from the time of the Renaissance – the idea of which is said to have been born in an Italian garden in the fifteenth century.

Italy to me means history, antiquity, museums, basilicas, glorious paintings and music, the beauty of sea-threatened Venice, and the wonders of Florence and Rome. It also means wonderful food (particularly pasta and delicious fish, once the pride of the Adriatic), singing colour (from the blue of the sky to the scarlet of the geraniums in windowboxes), and friendliness. I hope I have managed to capture some of these elements in my Italian arrangement.

Italy to me immediately suggests its long history – the glories of her art galleries and museums in almost every city, and the Vatican and innumerable beautiful churches – and this was the sort of impression I wanted to create for this arrangement, something old, gilded and timeless.

The accessories, as always, dictate the mood, and these must be combined and secured in place before the actual arrangement is begun. The main features here are the two large church candlesticks with the dripping candles at the top. (Many candles are dripless these days, but if you like the effect of drips – *I* do, it adds texture and shape, much more attractive than stark, 'nude' candles – take an old lit candle of the same colour and drip the wax down the side of the arrangement candles.) When the candlesticks were placed at their two different levels, I then encircled them with an old gilt oval frame (parts of which are visible at top and bottom of the arrangement). I added some of my favourite spelter ewers – looking as if they had just been lifted from an Italian museum – some wonderful gold tassels and some gold brocade. All these contribute to the luscious, rich and old feel I wanted for the group.

It wasn't difficult to find the sort of plant materials I needed. I wanted the flowers to look *regal*, so gladioli – as popular in Italy as with a certain Australian dame – were an obvious choice, here creating the spine and height of the arrangement. Carnations are also loved in Italy, so these have been included along with the lovely 'Sonia' roses, so prominent in the centre, and which are great favourites of many flower arrangers throughout the world. Among and between these are slotted two types of lily: the peachy pink one is called 'Pirate' - a delightful flower to use and grow – and the cream one is 'Mont Blanc', one of the most useful lilies of all for us flower arrangers.

Tucked into the centre there is some of the lovely 'Autumn Joy' sedum, with further additions consisting of grapes, plain green ivy, 'Goldheart' ivy, and wineberry foliage which almost looks like sprays of blackcurrant. This pours down towards the front, along with the lovely bronze colours of bergenia and peony foliages.

The whole bronzy look of the arrangement makes it the sort of thing that would have been appreciated – I hope! – in the courts of fifteenth- or sixteenth-century Italy.

I always like to use unlikely things, and this wrought-iron frame was thrown out by someone: I thought it had possibilities and, after storing it for six years, it has now come into its own. It reminds me rather of a balcony on some Italian villa, and my arrangement is going to be its 'windowbox'.

1 I wired the frame to a wrought-iron stand (the latter one of a few shoe stands thrown out by a shoe shop) and placed the whole thing on a piece of vitreolite (given me by a friend doing up his bathroom: 'Any use, Derek?'). In the centre of the frame there is a piece of soaked floral foam in its container, and the foliage outline is being created with aspidistra leaves flowing to the left, Mahonia japonica and camellia. (Here the frame is the height.) To hide the mechanics, there is a central rosette of geranium leaves.

2 Red carnations are very much associated with Italy, I think primarily because of their bright and exciting colour, and I've used them in a sweeping line, following that of the foliage, through from the right, coming out at the left.

3 The second flower placements are red 'Medallion' roses, again following the line already created. I have also added two red geraniums, both to link up with the leaves already used, and to further reinforce that Italian windowbox impression.

4 For a real touch of interest and a talking point, I have added an edible part to the arrangement – glorious red sweet peppers, cut in half lengthways to show the subtly coloured, seeded insides. These were mounted on to wooden skewers which made a stem to be pushed into the floral foam.

5 For a final presentation of the arrangement in all its glory, I added an extra cluster of peppers to bring visual weight into the lower part of the grouping.

CYPRUS

The divided island of Cyprus lies in the east of the Mediterranean, not far from the south coast of Turkey, and west of the war-torn coast of the Lebanon. The island consists of a central plain which rises to the Kyrenia range in the north and in the south and west to the Troödos Mountains. Like Malta, the other island state in the Mediterranean, Cyprus was fought over by many civilisations and in a sense still is, as the partition of the island in 1975 – the north to the Turks, the south to the Greeks – is still in force.

Cyprus is not a member of WAFA, but I have visited the island many times. There are many very enthusiastic island flower arrangers who have a good variety of natural plant materials to call upon. As far as flowers are concerned, in the foothills and plains wild flowers are everywhere – cistus (rock roses) of all varieties, centaurea, daisies of the chrysanthemum family, mignonette, and fragrant herbs. From the foliage point of view, there are things like *Arum maculatum*, the arrow-shaped leaves known as lords and ladies, myrtle, and the typical Mediterranean pines and cypresses.

When I first went to Cyprus, it was on holiday with my wife Pat. Just out of curiosity I phoned up a friend to see if anything was happening and yes, the Philanthese club of Nicosia was having a meeting that Thursday, with one of their own members demonstrating. I duly turned up, had tea, admired the stage all efficiently set up, and sat down. But oh no, I was told, we want *you* to demonstrate, we just couldn't miss the opportunity. If anyone was ever thrown in at the deep end it was me on that occasion. There were 40 members there, and I had five minutes to look at containers and accessories, flowers and foliage . . . However, as I've said on so many occasions, I've never been beaten yet, and I don't intend to be. So I took up the challenge, did about five arrangements and entertained them for about 1¼ hours. They thought it absolutely fantastic that I had performed off the cuff so to speak, the arrangements were all photographed, and two appeared in the local paper the following week.

The following year they invited me back formally, and I performed in the ballroom of the Nicosia Hilton before over 400 people, quite a change from the previous time. My friend Lito said she would translate for me and when I paused to let her do her stuff, she got more laughs than I did (I've always wondered whether she *added* to the stories).

MALTA

Malta is a small island in the Mediterranean, to the south of Sicily, and comprises the two main islands of Malta and Gozo, and the smaller Comino. Because of this position, it was a prize for many occupiers, latterly the Arabs (the language of Malta is a dialect of North Arabic with elements of Italian). The island was ceded to the British in 1814, and became an important air and naval base. For their heroic defence of the island from German attack during the Second World War (1940-2), the people of Malta were awarded the George Cross, the highest British decoration for civilian bravery.

Malta is generally low-lying, and its climate is hot, the *sirocco* blowing directly north from the Sahara. Because the island is so exposed, very few shrubs or plants can maintain a roothold on the scant gravelly soil. Neither are there any reserves of water to sustain the plants in summer – there are no lakes or rivers to speak of – and much of the winter rainfall simply runs into the sea. The most common shrub seen as hedging along roadsides and around the carefully tended small fields is actually a member of the cactus family, *Opuntia vulgaris*, the prickly pear or Barbary fig. This has become a virtual weed in many countries as it can be propagated with such ease.

Malta is a member of WAFA and has two flower-arranging societies, the Malta Flower Club itself, and the Malita Flower Club (Malita is the old name for Malta), with which I have most associations. I have demonstrated many times on the island and love visiting it because of the warmth of the people. Although the island doesn't have very much vegetation, the flowers that are grown there, some in private gardens or in pots on terraces or balconies, are quite magnificent, and it does me good, I feel, to see how some people can adapt, adopt and improve even without access to certain ingredients, like foliage, which I feel I couldn't live without. When I demonstrate there, I always take with me the largest box of foliage I can manage, and people descend on every leftover blade, be it of sansevieria or common or garden grass, like a plague of locusts!

I had a very interesting time once because the then President's wife was guest of honour at my demonstration. If I needed any more foliage during the week, she said, I was to come and pick from her garden. I duly went, but she had omitted to tell me that her garden was the Botanic Garden! I picked some wonderful things, much to the chagrin of the members who had never had the same opportunities!

My first impression on visiting Malta was the *colour* of the island: it all seemed to be one colour, the houses, the soil, the complete landscape (that of the inside of a Crunchie bar). To see it at sunset though, it is quite magnificent. This monotone impression introduces the other aspect of Malta, especially to us flower arrangers, and that is the lack of vegetation. Gozo, the other major island making up the Republic, has a mass of green, but Malta has none (did they chop all their trees down at some point in the past?). It's a great problem for the island flower arrangers, but they show great ingenuity, and come up with some wonderful ideas.

My principal aim in my Maltese arrangement was to reflect the great historic feel of the island. Because of its strategic position, it's been occupied many times, successively by the Phoenicians, Greeks, Carthaginians and Romans, and there are numerous sites and artefacts around the island. That's why I chose as my container a terracotta cherub head, which I thought very Romanesque in look. It's a wall mask container, and so had an open top into which I could wedge my soaked floral foam. To support the mask, I fixed it to a shaped wooden backing, spray-painted browny terracotta. (This was actually the middle part of a 1940s triple-mirror dressing-table, minus the mirror – I use everything!)

Because Malta is so steeped in tradition, I decided on a traditional arrangement. And because of the lack of foliage, I used that from house plants, as the local flower arrangers do, and some of the glorious flowers that are grown on the island.

The outline foliages flowing to the right and sweeping up to the left and top are aspidistra leaves, nephrolepis fern and hart's tongue fern. These create height and width. To left and right, as the flower part of the arrangement, there are peachy coral spray carnations, leading into coral-coloured frilly carnations. Recessed, there are some bronze spray chrysanthemums. The highlight flowers, used as a focal point, are 'Champagne' roses and cream 'Stirling Star' lilies.

The soft creamy and terracotta colours, as well as the container and accessories, completely sum up for me the antiquity, dryness and beauty of Malta.

SWITZERLAND

Switzerland is a land-locked country in western Europe, bordered to the north by the Federal Republic of Germany, to the north and west by France, to the south by Italy, and to the east by Austria and the tiny principality of Liechtenstein. The Jura Mountains of the north-west give way to a high plateau which then rises to the heights of the Alps in the south. The River Rhine and Lake Constance (or the Bodensee) form most of the border of the north and east, while in the south the River Rhône flows from the Alps through Lake Geneva (Lac Léman) into France. Switzerland was conquered several times in its history, becoming at one point a part of the Holy Roman Empire. The various cantons eventually joined to become a unified federal state. Switzerland remained neutral through both world wars, and is now the base of many international organisations, the Red Cross and the World Health Organisation among them.

That Switzerland was a member of WAFA came as a bit of a surprise – it means mountains and snow, watches and money to me. I suppose the main surprise lay in the fact that one doesn't automatically associate snow and mountains with flowers, although of course flowers can be imported from anywhere in the world if the desire is there. However, where there's a will there's a way, and there are a great number of domestic gardens, both large and small in Switzerland, although quite a few, I must admit, lie at an angle! The weather too is often a bit of a disadvantage for the gardener and the cultivation of flowers, because of course it's very cold in the winter, spring can often be very late, and much of the annual rainfall can appear in the middle of the summer.

However, there are really two climates in Switzerland in the botanical sense. In the summer, even quite high up, chalet balconies, and apartment roof gardens are aflame with pots and troughs of geraniums. The foothills drift with spring flowers like gentian and edelweiss, and gardens in and around the big cities such as Zürich and Geneva are brilliant with roses, camellia, and many of the same sorts of flowers and shrubs that are cultivated elsewhere in Europe. There are also quite a few Botanical Gardens in Switzerland which are magnificent – often specialising in orchids, succulents and cacti. There is even one which features sub-tropical plants collected from the Mediterranean, South America, South Africa and the Far East, which is situated on an island in Lake Maggiore.

But it is the small alpine plants that will always be most associated with Switzerland, and there are many Alpengärten or Alpine gardens in the country. These are landscaped, in their natural habitats in the mountains, thousands of feet above sea level. Plants with which we are familiar from alpinetums in the UK and other parts of Europe include androsace (rock jasmine), aquilegia (columbine), asters, dwarf conifers, dianthus (pinks), sedum, true geraniums or crane's bill, and, the prize of them all, the gentians and *Leontopodium alpinum*, the edelweiss. None of these would be useful in flower arranging, of course, but do think about 'arranging' them as growing plants in your rock garden or, better still, in a lovely display in an old stone trough in the garden.

My earliest recollection of Switzerland – for I haven't demonstrated there – is of a school trip in the mid 1950s. We stayed in Interlaken, then a delightful small town (*much* bigger now, I believe), and went on trips into the mountains. Even at that early age, I must have loved flowers, foliage and vegetation because my prime memory is of the wild flowers carpeting the meadows around Grindelwald. Perhaps it was in Switzerland that my future was decided!

Switzerland is not a country one naturally associates with flowers apart from, of course, the gentian and edelweiss, and the geraniums spilling out of windowboxes all through the summer. But what does readily spring to mind for everyone is snow, ice and winter sports, and thus I've created a cool, icy arrangement, using cool clear glass, one of my favourite mediums, and of which I have an enormous collection.

The base of the arrangement is a round piece of mirror tile which gives wonderful reflections. As I needed height for the idea, I used a clear glass spaghetti jar standing about 2 feet (60 cm) in height (I can find a use for most things). The two glass containers, the tops of which look rather like icicles pointing to the heavens, I found in a Spanish market.

My greatest problem was how to get some form of foam holder between the top of the spaghetti jar and the base of the top candle holder. This I managed to do by using a clear glass sugar basin from the kitchen cupboard. I wanted something that would blend in and not be visible when the arrangement was complete, that would sit on the top of the jar, plus hold the candle holder and the foam. The lower placement had to be considered at the same time, so I used another, very much smaller, glass dish and a small piece of floral foam.

The first placements were the white-painted wires sweeping in separate arcs from top arrangement to bottom arrangement. Following these lines are sprays of ivy which I slightly frosted with sparkling spray paint, together with nephrolepis fern, the natural foliage part of the arrangement. Sprays of fern in the bottom part of the arrangement provide the linkage between the two parts of the group.

I found some very interesting plastic filigreed leaves which were in silver and ice-blue centred sprays, and I used these to both left and right of the top arrangement, and to complement that, a little in the bottom arrangement. The final foliage placements were sprays of silver lurex philodendron foliage.

To bring the centre part of both arrangements together, clear glass baubles were used in clusters before the final placements of fresh white carnations.

The wires arching down the arrangement already remind me of ski tracks on a snowy slope, but to further reinforce this cool Swiss feel, I added a cluster of glass icicles at the left to complement them. For a final icy touch, I laid chunks of rough clear glass between the elements of the lower arrangement, which wonderfully reflect in the mirror.

A cool icy arrangement, using mainly artificial materials, to echo the snow-and-winter-sports image Switzerland has for me.

PLANT GLOSSARY

Acacia (Leguminosae) The wattle, native to Australia and Tasmania, belongs to a genus of about 800 species of shrubs and trees. It bears short-lived, minute, petal-less flowers in globular clusters, and those of *A.dealbata*, the silver wattle, are the florist's mimosa. One wattle yields gum arabic, another a variety of lac, and several Australian wattle barks are rich in tannin, so are used in commerce. The name comes from the Greek for the gum arabic tree, derived from *akis*, a sharp point.

Acer (Aceraceae) The maple, a large family of deciduous trees, originated from China and Japan, but has now spread across the northern hemisphere. Size varies from shrub to large tree; leaf and key shapes vary too. In North America maples are large, and they are the trees which turn New England in the fall into an artist's palette of colours. *Acer saccharum*, the sugar maple, is the emblem of Canada. In Europe the maple is represented by the 'weed' sycamore and the field maple. In the East, particularly Japan, maples are smaller and more intricate. *Acer palmatum 'Atropurpureum'* – the

bloodleaf Japanese maple – is the most popular in Europe, and makes wonderful foliage. Do not pick it too young, though: if picked later on in the year, it will last extremely well.

Alstroemeria (Alstroemeriaceae) The Peruvian lily belongs to a genus of 50 species of South American lilies with tuberous roots. They are generally grown under glass and there are many hybrids. They are very long-lasting when cut. The roots were eaten by the natives. The name comes from that of a friend of Linnaeus, Baron Claus Alstroemer.

Amaranthus (Amaranthaceae) A genus of over 60 species of annuals, some grown for their bright foliage, others for their tassel or plume-like flowers. They originate from tropical America. *A. caudatus* is familiarly known as 'love-lies-bleeding'. Many species are useful as foliage as the ovate leaves, particularly of *A. tricolor*, are scarlet or crimson, overlaid with yellow, bronze and green. I grow this in my own garden, and have managed to get it about 15–18 inches (38–45 cm) high; that used in the arrangement for Eire (see page 107) came from Holland

and was about 3 feet (90 cm) in length! The tender leaves and shoots of some amaranthus are cooked and eaten in curries, or substituted for spinach in the tropics; some seeds are ground into flour. The name comes from the Greek *amarantos*, everlasting – amaranthus lasts well in water when cut, and can be dried.

Amaryllis (Amaryllidaceae) A genus with a single bulbous species. *A. belladonna*, the belladonna lily, originated in South Africa. It has strap-shaped leaves and red to pale pink trumpet-shaped flowers on bare stems; these flowers vary in number from about three to twelve. The plant needs protection in temperate climates, and can be grown in a pot. It is long lasting, and is named after the shepherd in classical poetry.

Ananas (Bromeliaceae) A genus of five species of evergreen plants, native to tropical America. All are terrestrial, and one member of the family is *A. comosus* or *sativus*, the edible pineapple. They are available as house plants, and I find them very useful in a multitude of ways. They have sharp-toothed and spined leaves in a loose rosette and *A. comosus 'Variegatus'* has a centre which turns red. I put some out in the garden in the long hot summer of 1989 where they flourished and produced babies! Some ananas plants, in the Philippines particularly, yield a fibre which is used in cloth.

Anthurium (Araceae) The anthurium lily – also known as flamingo or oil-cloth flower, or painter's palette – belongs to a genus of over 500 species of evergreens, native to South America. They have striking flower-petal-like spathes, waxy red or white, with a cylindrical 3 inch (8 cm) long spadix (which actually bears the tiny flowers); the leaves are large and satiny, heart of arrowhead shaped, and these can be up to 8 inches (20 cm) long. In the wild they can be epiphytic or terrestrial; away from their native warmth and humidity, they have to be greenhouse cultivated, and can be bought in pots. They last well. The name comes from the Greek *anthos*, flower, and *oura*, tail, referring to the shape of the flower spadix.

Aralia, see **Fatsia**

Aspidistra (Liliaceae) The familiar house plant comes from a genus of eight evergreen species, originally from Asia. The leaves are dark green, oblong and lanceolate, and can be up to 20 inches (50 cm) long; a variegated variety has white to cream striped leaves. The flowers, which seldom appear, are purple, insignificant and close to the ground. It is also known as the cast-iron plant because it can withstand the poorest of conditions – those dark Victorian parlours, for instance. The leaves are useful as fresh foliage, but they can also be glycerined, dried and bleached. The name comes from the Greek, *aspidion*, small round shield, referring to the shape of the stigma.

Astilbe (Saxifragaceae) A genus of 25 species of herbaceous perennials native to China and Japan. They have mid to deep green divided foliage and colourful feathery plumes of flowers. For use in arrangements, astilbe needs quite a lot of conditioning, I have discovered: it's a lot better if you take all the foliage off and just let all the moisture go to the flowers.

Azalea (Ericaceae) Azaleas are included in the large genus *Rhododendron*, the florist's pot azalea usually being *Rhododendron simsii*. Most rhododendrons originate from Japan, Korea and China. Azaleas are small shrub hybrids, with pretty flowers and glossy leaves, ideal house plants (and mostly grown in Belgium).

Bamboo Bamboos are tropical grasses, having hard-walled stems with ringed joints. They vary considerably in size and character, some growing to only a few feet in height, others to 100 feet (30 metres) or more. They grow all over the world, mainly at height and in the tropics – *Bambusa aurea* in Japan, *Dendrocalamus giganteus* in Burma, for instance – but some can be garden-grown in temperate zones. I love the look of bamboo, and use it a lot: thin stained lengths as in the Jamaican arrangement on page 57; thick lengths carved into a container as in the Japanese arrangement on page 63 (along with a bamboo table and screen). The plant pot use of thick bamboo is very traditional; in bamboo-growing countries it is also used as a building material, as scaffolding, and to build road bridges. One found in Hong Kong is known as punt-pole bamboo for perhaps obvious reasons. Split bamboo is woven into things like mats, baskets and hats.

For the South African arrangement I even found another part of the bamboo to use. When in a friend's garden in Africa, I noticed the triangular leaf-like growths or sheaths at the rings on a 9 inch (28 cm) thick bamboo: these I carefully removed, and have used in the arrangement in reverse, the wide side (which would have been at the ring on the bamboo) to the outside, the point into the centre of the arrangement and in the floral foam. Incidentally, I was told to wash my hands thoroughly after handling these: the inner surfaces were covered in a sort of pollen, and this apparently is itch-inducing, used by locals just as itching powder is in the West!

Banksia (Proteaceae) A genus of 50 species, originating chiefly from Western Australia, varying from prostrate shrubs in which flower spikes rise from the ground, to large-growing trees. They are often known as Australian honeysuckle trees as the nectar is very attractive to small birds. They are named after Sir Joseph Banks, the English naturalist (1743-1820) who sailed with Captain Cook on his first voyage (and later became director of Kew). People often confuse the dense flower heads with those of the protea. I brought some back with me from Australia in the green state but they dried well, keeping their lovely bronzy brown colouring.

Begonia (Begoniaceae) A genus of over 2,000 species and hybrids, some grown for their flowers, some for their decorative foliage. They are greenhouse or pot plants in temperate zones. Because the genus is so large, it is usually sub-divided into three groups – fibrous-rooted, rhizomatous, or tuberous. The latter originate from the East, the others from South America. The *Begonia rex-cultorum –* king, rex or painted-leaf begonia - has asymmetrical heart-shaped leaves, up to 12 inches (30 cm) long and 10 inches (25 cm) wide, with spectacular colourings, very useful in many arrangements. Pale pink or white flowers sometimes appear on mature plants in summer.

Berberis (Berberidaceae) The barberry belongs to a genus of over 400 species of deciduous and evergreen shrubs native to the East and South America. They are usually spiny and easy on the whole to grow in temperate zones. The glossy leaves of the evergreen varieties grow in rosette clusters and are useful for many arrangements; the deciduous species are particularly valuable to us in autumn for their abundance of scarlet berries.

Bergenia (Saxifragaceae) A genus of six hardy herbaceous perennials native to Asia. They have glossy green, large, leathery leaves which sometimes become red in the autumn, and the plants are worth growing in any flower-arranger's garden as ground cover, for their big heads of flowers, and for arrangement foliage. I like particularly the giant saxifrage, elephant's ears, and *B. purpurascens* 'Ballawley', a hybrid which has larger leaves and flowers than its parents. The plant is named after one Karl August von Bergen, a professor in Frankfurt in the eighteenth century.

Bougainvillea (Nyctaginaceae) A genus of 18 species of climbing deciduous plants native to South America. They must be greenhouse or pot grown in temperate zones. The flowers are insignificant but are surrounded by brilliantly coloured papery bracts that persist – thus the familiar name of 'paper flower'. I was introduced to the idea of arranging bougainvillea when in South Africa, having thought up till then that it was unarrangeable. The variety there called 'Natalia', with peach to bronze colouring, took up water extremely well after all the foliage was stripped off. It has to be a fairly mature flower, though. The plant is named after Louis Antoine de Bougainville, an eighteenth-century traveller.

Camellia (Theaceae) A genus of over 75 species of evergreen shrubs and trees, native to Asia. (A member of the camellia family is the tea bush, *C.thea*.) A popular house plant because of its cup- or bowl-shaped flowers, I value it mainly for its handsome glossy foliage. When cut, this is one of the longest-lasting of foliages.

Carnation, see **Dianthus**

Chincherinchee, see **Ornithogalum**

Chrysanthemum (Compositae) A genus of more than 200 species of annuals, shrubs and herbaceous perennials. They originate from China and Japan, and those popularly known now as florists' chrysanthemums are divided into several groups according to blooms, one of which includes my favourite spray chrysanthemum. The flower is very much valued in Japan (see page 61). In ancient China, tradition had it that the dew collected from the flowers preserved and

restored vitality; eating the flowers might confer immortality. The name comes from the Greek *chrysos*, gold, and *anthos*, flower.

Clematis (Ranunculaceae) A genus of over 200 species of woody, flowering climbers, which come variously from Europe, Asia and China. It's a useful plant for a flower-arranger's garden, as it quickly climbs walls and trellising; the pendant bell flowers are good looking and the dark green sprays of leaves, conditioned well, make a good lasting foliage. The old man's beard or traveller's joy which clings to bushes and trees, its ripe fluffy fruits looking like cotton wool, is a European native clematis, *C. vitalba*.

Coccoloba uvifera (Polygonaceae) There are several species of sea grape, and they vary in habit depending on environment: those near the sea, for example, are shrubby and low but, inland, trees can reach heights of about 50 feet (15 metres). The leaves are flat, rounded and up to 8 inches (20 cm) across, smooth and shiny with reddish veins. The plants produce flowers and fruits (sour but edible) in their native habitat, the Caribbean and coastal South America – and may, some believe, have been the first plant seen by Columbus on his fifteenth-century voyages of discovery. In the wild, the hollow leaf stems often contain colonies of ants.

The leaves can be dried easily, and are very useful indeed in arrangements. They can also be dyed.

Codiaeum (Euphorbiaceae) Croton belongs to a genus of 15 species of evergreen shrubs, native to the East. They are available in Europe as house plants, appreciated mainly for their ornamental leaves. There is a wide variation in colouring and shape of leaves, and they are variously lobed. It is sickening for a flower arranger to see these plants growing happily in other places such as South Africa and the Caribbean where they are used as hedges. Here you do well to get a pot plant to reach 2 feet (60 cm), and it's not a case of cutting a huge piece off a hedge, the decision is whether to take one or two leaves!

Cordyline (Agavaceae) A genus of 15 species of evergreen palm-like shrubs and trees, native to Asia and Australasia, grown for their handsome foliage. In pots they reach 2-3 feet (60-90 cm), in their natural habitats, some reach 25 feet (7.5 metres)! They are often listed as Dracaenas. *C. australis* is also known as cabbage palm or palm lily, and is hardy enough to grow in western Europe, including southern Ireland and Cornwall. It is thought to have acquired the name 'cabbage' from early settlers, who used the tender young plants as vegetables, much as hearts of palm are eaten in many parts of the world. *C. terminalis* is also known as the goodluck plant, Polynesian *ti* plant or tree of kings. The name cordyline comes from the Greek *kordyle*, club or cudgel, thought to refer to the shape of the roots.

Cortaderia (Gramineae) Pampas grass belongs to a genus of 15 species of perennial evergreen grasses, native to the Argentine. They are a must in any flower-arranger's garden as a feature plant, both for their strip-like foliage (be careful, it's very sharp on the edges), and for their silky, silvery flowering plumes. You need space though, and they can grow to 6-7 feet (1.8-2 metres) high. Cut the plumes young to hang and dry, and they can also be bought dyed.

Corylus (Betulaceae) There are several varieties of hazel, most of them valued for their catkins and nuts, but I find *C. avellana 'Contorta'*, the contorted hazel, the most useful in flower arrangements. It's the sort of plant, however, that needs to be tucked away somewhere as I think it looks most unattractive when in full leaf in spring and summer. In the other two seasons the sinuous branches are wonderful to see, and indeed I do most of my pruning before the leaves appear. Put it where you can easily do your picking, but not necessarily where you have to look at it!

Cotoneaster (Rosaceae) A genus of about 50 species of hardy evergreen and deciduous shrubs native to the East. Good for hedging, they have flowers followed by wonderfully conspicuous red-orange berries in the autumn. The name comes from the Latin *cotonea*, quince, and *aster*, kind of.

Crabapple, see **Malus**

Croton, see **Codiaeum**

Cucurbita (Cucurbitaceae) Ornamental gourds belong to a group of herbaceous climbing plants, and their edible relations are squash, pumpkin, marrow, etc. They are native to tropical America, and come in a variety of sizes, shapes and colours – apple-shaped, egg, pear, Hercules' club, cup and saucer, and small warted. Seeds are available for greenhouse cultivation, but they can be bought, some already dried, from markets and flower-arranging shops. Some are varnished, *not* a good idea if they are not fully dried inside. You can collect them on holidays abroad, picking them fresh and allowing them to dry slowly – patience is required, though, as it can take up to twelve months. Do not puncture them at any time or the flesh will rot. Keep in a dry place and, after use in an arrangement, dry carefully, again to avoid rot.

In their native habitats, gourds, particularly the calabash gourd (*Crescentia cujete*), are used as water-carrying vessels. Calabashes come from trees about 30 feet (9 metres) high, and the flowers are pollinated by bats. Snake gourds can be up to 6 feet (1.8 metres) long, and the familiar bath loofah is the fibrous skeleton of the loofah or sponge gourd.

Cycas (Cycadaceae) Cycad palms are not in fact palms, although they are palm-like, but belong to a genus of some 100 species thought to be among the most primitive seed-bearing plants still in existence. They are often the 'palms' grown in foreign hotel gardens, and the house plant, *C. revoluta*, sago palm, is a cycad. The fern-like leaves are useful in many ways. The name comes from the Greek *kykas*, used by Theophrastus to mean a palm.

Cymbidium (Orchidaceae) A genus of about 50 species of orchids which grow in their native habitat in the tropics, east and west, as epiphytes. In cultivation they are terrestrial, and can be found as house plants. There are many colours and sizes available, and they are easy to grow under glass. The flowers – useful in so many arrangements – are long lasting on the plant and when cut. The name comes from the Greek *kymbe*, boat, referring to the hollow recess in the lip of the flowers.

Dahlia (Compositae) A genus of about 20 species and innumerable hybrids, native originally to Mexico. The very showy flowers are useful in many arrangements. They are named after an eighteenth-century botanist, Anders Dahl, a pupil of Linnaeus.

Delphinium (Ranunculaceae) A genus of 350 species of annuals and herbaceous perennials native to the East. The tall spikes of flowers come in a wide range of colours, and look beautiful in the garden or in arrangements. The name comes from the Greek *delphis*, dolphin.

Dianthus caryophyllus (Caryophyllaceae) Carnations belong to a genus of about 300 species of annual and evergreen perennials which also include pinks and sweet williams. They hybridise readily and are one of the most useful of florists' flowers, in single and spray forms.

Dracaena (Agavaceae) A genus of 40 species of evergreen shrubby plants, native to Africa, which are grown for their foliage. They have sword-like or laurel-like leaves, can be palm-like, and are often confused with Cordylines. *D. sanderana*, Belgian evergreen or gold-dust dracaena, is particularly spectacular. The name comes from the Greek *drakaina*, dragon's blood, which refers to the red dye or varnish obtained from some species, including a large tree, *D. draco* or dragon tree (one in Tenerife was thought by some to be one of the oldest vegetable inhabitants of the earth).

Echeveria (Crassulaceae) A fleshy genus of 200 species of house plants and greenhouse perennials. They are succulents, native to Mexico, with beautifully and variously coloured rosettes of waxy and bloomed leaves, which range considerably in size. They have bell flowers on arching stems. They are named after one Athanasio Echeverria Godoy, an eighteenth-century botanical artist.

Eucalyptus (Myrtaceae) About three-quarters of all the forest trees in Australia are evergreen eucalypts, known as gum trees. There are about 600 species in Australia – the snow gum, the lemon-scented, the blue and so on – and the young foliage is most useful in arrangements: the leaves are often waxy, greyish white, almost silvery. These can be dried and glycerined. Hardwood eucalypts now grow in most sub-tropical areas, and some are hardy enough for western Europe.

I've also found eucalyptus *bark* very useful. This is as deciduous as most trees' leaves, and flakes off in patterns. To use it (in the South African arrangement, see page 25), I wound each piece of bark around my fingers tightly, tied it with string, and then soaked it in water for 24 hours. After drying in the sun, the string was removed, leaving lovely spiral whirls. (The same can be done with cane, as in the Mexican step-by-step arrangement.)

Euonymus (Celastraceae) A genus of about 170 species of deciduous and evergreen shrubs and trees, native to China and Japan. They are grown mainly for the autumn colours of the foliage and the fruit (the flowers are inconspicuous). *E. europaea* is the common spindle tree, which produces tiny pink fruits with orange seeds: these are loved by birds, but are violently purgative to man (used as such in folk medicine, as well as against head lice, thus another name, louseberries!). The wood is used for spindles, skewers, toothpicks (another early name for the tree was prickwood), pegs, keys and knitting needles. *E. japonicus* is the plant commonly found in pots, and has many variations in colouring – 'Albo-marginatus', white margins, and 'Aureo-variegatus' with bright yellow blotches.

Euphorbia (Euphorbiaceae) A genus of some 2,000 species of shrubs found all over the world, some of which are succulent, and a genus which includes the Mexican pot plant, *E. pulcherrima*, the poinsettia. As on the familiar poinsettia, the flowers are small and insignificant, the bracts surrounding them much more conspicuous. They were named after Euphorbus, physician to a King of Mauritania.

Fatsia (Araliaceae) *Fatsia japonica* (also known as *Aralia japonica*) is the only species in the genus. It is an evergreen shrub native to Japan (the name comes from the Japanese *fat si*). It has been used for over a hundred years as a handsome, quick-growing house plant. It has large, nicely glossy palmate leaves, umbels of flowers on outdoor plants (needing wall protection other than in the south), and black ivy-like berries. It's a very useful plant for any flower-arranger's garden, particularly variegated types.

Ferns There are about 10,000 species of fern, and many can be found in pots. My favourites for foliage use are the sword fern, *Nephrolepis cordifolia*, and the hart's tongue fern, *Phyllitis scolopendrium*. *Nephrolepis* comes from Greek, *nephros*, kidney, and *lepis*, scale; *phyllitis* comes from the Greek *phyllon*, leaf. Nephrolepis is fringed and feathery; phyllitis leaves are entire and strap-like. For use in arrangements, I recommend that garden ferns, of whatever variety, are not picked until fairly late on in the season, never before August anyway. The way to remember this is to look at the spores on the back of the ferns, part of their unique manner of reproduction: when these have changed from green to brown, the ferns are mature and ready for picking and, in many cases, will last well for weeks.

Gaultheria (Ericaceae) A genus of some 200 species of evergreen flowering shrubs native to many regions. G. *shallon*, sometimes known as Salop, comes from western North America, and has mid to dark green ovate leaves; pink or white racemes of flowers are followed by purple-black berries.

Geranium, see **Pelargonium**

Gerbera (Compositae) A genus of about 70 species of perennial and flowering plants native to the Transvaal. The daisy-like flowers come in a multitude of colours and last extremely well as cut flowers. Gerberas are also known as the Transvaal daisy and Barberton daisy (G. *jamesonii*). One of the things that interested me on my trip to South Africa was that the gerberas do not grow as big there, despite being native, as they do commercially in Europe. The biggest flower was probably 2-2½ inches (5-6 cm) across: here I've used them as big as 5 inches (13 cm).

Gladiolus (Iridaceae) A genus of some 300 species of bulbous flowering plants native to Africa and Asia. There are numerous hybrids, which produce a multitude of colours. I find

the dark green leaves as useful as the flowers.

Gourds, see **Cucurbita**

Griselinia (Cornaceae) A genus of six species of slightly tender evergreen shrubs or trees native to New Zealand. It can be used as hedging in southern coastal areas, but many people complain that it is too tender for Britain. I grow it successfully though. The big leathery leaves are very useful as foliage both in gardens and flower arrangements.

Gums, see **Eucalyptus**

Guzmania (Bromeliaceae) A genus of about 100 species of evergreen perennials native to tropical America and the Caribbean, and grown in temperate climates in greenhouse or pots. In the wild they are usually epiphytic. Rosettes of glossy, smooth-edged leaves form water-holding vases. The central floral bracts (surrounding tiny, insignificant flowers) are brilliant in colour, and last for many months. The name derives from that of the eighteenth-century Spanish botanist, Anastasio Guzman.

Gypsophila (Caryophyllaceae) A genus of some 100 species of delicately flowered plants. The one I find most useful is G. *paniculata* 'Bristol Fairy', which has double white flowers.

Hazel, see **Corylus**

Hebe (Scrophulariaceae) A genus of about 100 species of hardy evergreen flowering shrubs native to New Zealand. They are good foliage plants, with green or variegated, glossy, scale-like leaves, and interesting flowers.

Hedera (Araliaceae) Ivy is a genus of 15 species of hardy evergreen climbers, which grow in many places around the world. Ivies are very good plants for a flower-arranger's garden: they thrive in both sun and shade, and can grow in pots and up trellising (they're good house plants too). Sweeps of those prettily shaped and coloured leaves add to so many of my arrangements. Ivy is long lasting, too, as a cut foliage.

Helichrysum (Compositae) A genus of 500 species of flowering shrubs and herbaceous perennials and annuals native to many parts of the world. The daisy-like flowers of the annual species (*H. bracteatum*) are known as everlasting or straw flowers, because they dry so successfully. Another useful helichrysum is *H. petiolatum*: the stems and foliage, covered in a dense felt of white hairs, make beautiful curving shapes when cut. The name comes from the Greek *helios*, sun, and *chrysos*, golden.

Heliconia (Scitamineae) A shrub native to tropical America which has large handsome broad leaves and coloured flower and fruit spikes or inflorescences, which, in the wild, often harbour snakes and centipedes. They are available as cut flowers which last well, but they can also be dried (and painted, as the hanging heliconia in the Jamaican arrangement, see page 57).

Helleborus (Ranunculaceae) A genus of some 20 species of hardy evergreen and deciduous plants native to Europe. They are winter flowering, long lasting when cut, and include the Christmas rose (*H. niger*) and the Lenten rose (*H. orientalis*). The cup-shaped flowers of *H. corsicus* – which are yellow-green in colour – are particularly good for the flower arranger, as are the green leaves, and are easily grown in the garden.

Hosta (Liliaceae) A genus of 20 or so species of hardy herbaceous perennials native to Japan. They are grown for their large attractive leaves and their nodding trumpet-like flowers. I grow a variety in my garden as they make such good flower-arranging foliage: their size ranges from 2-20 inches (5-50 cm) in length, and the colours vary from lime green to deep blue-grey. I grow them in borders and in some of my many containers. Once established, they can be left undisturbed as clumps actually improve with age. Good varieties are *H. albo-marginata,*

H. sieboldiana and *H. fortunei* 'Albopicta'. Known also as the plantain lily, they are named for Nicholaus Tomas Host, an early nineteenth-century Austrian physician.

Hydrangea (Hydrangeaceae) A genus of about 80 species of deciduous and evergreen flowering shrubs and climbers, native to Asia. The common hortensia or mop-head can be found in pots, but is beautifully pink or blue in many European gardens (depending on acidity or alkalinity of soil). The lacecap hydrangea is a climber. In the autumn the hortensias turn some wonderfully offbeat colours. Those used in the Eire arrangement were pink during the hot summer of 1989 then turned that glorious green. Hydrangeas dry well – simply stick into a piece of drifoam, or leave in an arrangement. Only pick them, however, when the flowers, the tight little ball-shaped centres *inside* the coloured bracts, have 'gone over', leaving a spike. If you pick before then, the hydrangea will be too immature, and the drying process will be unsuccessful. The name comes from the Greek *hydro*, water, and *angeion*, vessel, referring to the cup-shaped fruits.

Hypoestes (Acanthaceae) Shrubs available as pot plants with attractively pink-spotted leaves. They can develop insignificant flowers. They are also known variously as baby's tears, freckle face and polka-dot plant.

Iris (Iridaceae) A genus of 300 plants native to the northern hemisphere. There are many hybrids. They are excellent for a flower-arranger's garden, not just for their pretty flowers, but for their sword-shaped leaves, which are very useful in arrangements.

Ivy, see **Hedera**

Ligustrum (Oleaceae) Privet comes from a genus of about 40-50 species of hardy deciduous and evergreen flowering shrubs and small trees native to Japan and Korea. Usually grown as hedging, they are useful too for the flower arranger because of their leaf colourings – particularly that of *L. ovalifolium* 'Aureo-marginatum', golden privet (green with yellow borders).

Lilium (Liliaceae) A genus of 80 species of bulbous plants which are found in the wild in temperate zones in Europe, China, Japan, etc. The madonna lily (*L. candidum*) is thought to have been cultivated for some 3,000 years, but there are now many variations and hybrids. Because of this, lilies are classified into nine divisions, among them Asiatic hybrids (eg 'Enchantment') and true species and their botanical forms and varieties (eg *longiflorum*, the Easter lily). I grow a great many lilies – about 30 varieties – in my own garden, among them 'Chinook' and 'Mont Blanc'. The latter is wonderful: I've had the bulbs for over five years and they produce masses of flowers every year without any bother. Others I use in arrangements are 'Stargazer, 'Stirling Star', 'Prominence', 'Pirate' and 'Connecticut King'. In China and Japan they cultivate the bulbs of lilies for edible and medicinal as well as floral purposes.

See also **Alstroemeria** and **Anthurium.**

Lonicera (Caprifoliaceae) Honeysuckle belongs to a genus of 200 species of shrubs and woody climbers, native to several parts of the northern hemisphere. The flowers on many are quite enchanting as well as fragrant, but the foliage of such as *L. nitida*, being evergreen, is very effective in flower arrangements. A golden-leaved variety, 'Baggesen's Gold', I like particularly, but it needs to be grown in full sun.

Mahonia (Berberidaceae) A genus of 70 species of hardy evergreen shrubs native to North America and China, with good foliage, yellow flowers, and berries. *M. japonica* has large spiny leaves and drooping flowering racemes. The plants are useful for the flower-arranger's garden not just because of the foliage colour

in the autumn, but because of the berries, which are green in spring, ripening to blue-black, sometimes deep purple. The plant was named for a late eighteenth-century horticulturalist, Bernard Mahon.

Malus (Rosaceae) Crabapples belong, naturally, to the apple family. The trees or shrubs are grown mainly for ornamental or garden purposes – the flowers *and* fruits are colourful – but the fruits can be made into a jelly. A number of the species most useful in flower arranging are from Japan.

Maple, see **Acer**

Moluccella (Labiatae) A genus of four species of annual and perennial plants, native to western Asia. *M. laevis* (bells of Ireland or shell-flower) has light green rounded leaves, a white fragrant flower spike and a shell-like green calyx. Moluccella can be used fresh or dried.

Monstera (Araceae) This popular house plant belongs to a genus of 50 species of evergreen climbers with aerial roots. *M. deliciosa* comes from Mexico where it can scale trees to a height of 20 feet (6 metres). The leaves when young are whole, but as they mature, they become perforated which accounts for other popular names such as splitleaf and Swiss cheese plant. (These perforations are thought to help the wild plants survive tropical winds, thus another name, the hurricane plant.) The plant has a flowering spathe and a cone-like fruit which is eaten in the tropics.

Ornithogalum (Liliaceae) A genus of 150 species of bulbous plants found in Europe, Africa and Asia. Many are tender and have star-shaped flowers (O. *umbellatum*, star of Bethlehem, for instance), but O. *thyrsoides*, the chincherinchee from South Africa, has a cup-shaped flower and strap leaves. The flower lasts well when cut. The name comes from the Greek *ormis*, bird, and *gala*, milk, because the flowers are usually white. All parts of the plant are poisonous.

Paeonia (Paeoniaceae) The peony comes from a genus of some 30 species of plants grown for their showy flowers and very useful foliage. They were named after a Greek physician called Paeon.

Palms (Palmae) There are many types of palm, which include familiar tropical trees such as the coconut and date palms, and numerous others seen mostly in Europe as house plants. They are all tropical, evergreen, and have characteristically unbranched trunks. There are two major types of palm leaves – palmate or fan-shaped, and pinnate or feather-shaped – and I find them all very useful, gathering whenever I can when abroad, bringing home green and then letting

them dry. Palmetto, or cabbage, palms are particularly useful.

I also use other parts of palms. A hollowed out coconut shell (from *Cocos nucifera*) was a useful container in the Jamaican arrangement on page 57; the fruit-bearing branches of the date palm (*Phoenix dactylifera*) make spectacular 'foliage' in the Bermudan arrangement on page 49. Another less obvious palm 'product' for flower arranging is the spathe base left after an old leaf drops off. This curls over into a good shape and often drops off by itself or is cut off when the trees are pruned. I've got quite a few, and very useful they are too.

Pampas grass, see **Cortaderia**

Pelargonium (Geraniaceae) A genus of 400 species of evergreen and deciduous shrubs, native to South Africa. The pelargoniums commonly called geraniums should not be confused with the European genus *Geranium*. Geraniums are the quintessential windowbox flower, and have prettily marked and shaped leaves; these are fragrant and are distilled into essential oil used in medicine and perfumery.

Peony, see **Paeonia**

Pineapple, see **Ananas**

Pinus (Coniferae) A genus of evergreen conical trees which includes firs, spruces, cedars, larches and hemlocks. There are many varieties throughout the world, and they are particularly appreciated in Japan. The pines of North America include the sugar pine, the Ponderosa and pitch pines, and the Douglas fir. Mexico, too, has quite a few. In Europe, we have among others the Scots, Bosnian, umbrella, Corsican and Aleppo pines. The foliage and cones of pines can be very useful to the flower arranger, and many are very decorative in the garden. But pine 'driftwood', such as you might find lurking in an old pine forest somewhere, can be invaluable as a 'container' or base for an arrangement. Unlike other driftwoods it does not get eaten by worms – because of the resin perhaps? – and thus you'll have no worry at all about bringing it into your home.

Privet, see **Ligustrum**

Protea (Proteaceae) The family of *Proteaceae* consists of about 60 genera and 1,400 species, and is spread over Australia, Africa, South America, etc. Out of the 13 genera of Africa, 10 occur only in the south-western Cape, and two out of the remaining three – *Leucospermum* and *Protea* – are found mainly in South Africa. All 47 species of *Leucospermum* occur within South Africa, and of the 130 species of *Protea*, 100 occur in South Africa with the others extending as far north as

Nigeria and Ethiopia. The evergreen trees and shrubs have broad simple leaves and small white, pink, yellow or orange flowers that are grouped into showy cup-shaped clusters up to 12 inches (30 cm) across, and surrounded by whorls of coloured bracts. It is a tremendous family, chief of which is *P. cynaroides*, the king protea, the floral emblem of South Africa. They are greatly loved by all flower arrangers chiefly because they dry so well and are so decorative. I actually let my fresh proteas (they're easy to buy) dry in the arrangement: as the other flowers and foliages are 'going over', I just let the floral foam dry out and the proteas dry down beautifully. You could also put the stem of the flower in a bottle to support the head while drying: if you hang the flower, the head closes up and they don't look so attractive then. They turn various shades of cream to brown when dried. Sadly, the tiny, feathery pincushion proteas – *Leucospermum cordifolium* – cannot be dried.

Rhododendron (Ericaceae) A genus of at least 500 species of evergreen and deciduous trees and shrubs native to Asia. This includes *Azalea*, formerly treated as a different genus, and which is the 'rhododendron' available as house plants. The flowers vary in size and colours, and the glossy leaves, often variegated – as in *R. ponticum* 'Variegatum' – make very good foliage. Rhododendrons have become weeds in many parts of the world where they have been introduced – in Snowdonia, for instance. The name comes from the Greek *rhodos*, rose, and *dendron*, tree.

Rosa (Rosaceae) There are at least 250 distinct species of rose today, with many hybrids, which were cultivated over the years from old 'parents' such as *R. gallica*, *R. centifolia* and, later, *R. chinensis*. Roses and their foliage are invaluable in many flower arrangements. I use many florists' roses, among them 'Champagne', 'Gerdo', 'Frisco', 'Medallion', 'Sonia', 'Handel' and 'Mercedes'. *Rosa rubrifolia* is a species rose, a wild rose essentially, which is related to *R. canina*, the dog rose. I use it as foliage because it has violet-flushed stems and grey-mauve leaves. *Rosa rugosa* is also a species rose, with wrinkled foliage, solitary pink, fragrant flowers, and round orange hips which appear in the autumn.

Rowan, see **Sorbus**

Rubus (Rosaceae) A genus of 250 hardy climbing evergreen and deciduous shrubs, usually prickly, which include brambles, blackberries and raspberries. Some are ornamental shrubs, grown for their foliage stems. *R. phoenicolasius*, the Japanese wineberry, has mid green leaves which are white beneath, and stems

bearing edible fruit which look more like sea urchins than berries! They make lovely sweeps in an arrangement.

Salix (Salicaceae) Willows grow all over the world in temperate zones, most famously in China. There are two members of the family, willows and poplars, and both have male and female catkins on different trees. Willows are useful in flower arranging in all sorts of ways. The white willow, *S. alba*, has coloured shoots when young, brightest in the first winter, and these must be cut to encourage bushy growth (think of all those pollarded willows one sees). These shoots or stems obviously can be useful in arrangements. The twisted willow of Peking – *S. matsudana* 'Tortuosa' – has those curling twisting branches which I find so visually effective in many circumstances. Willows often become fasciated – when a normally cylindrical stem or other surface becomes flattened or ribbon-like – and pieces of this old wood are wonderful as accessories or containers (see page 26). The main use of willow worldwide, however (apart from making cricket bats), is in wickerwork, the pliant, durable and light shoots making such things as beehives, cradles, lobster pots and, above all, baskets. I love using the latter in arrangements, as I do rings of wicker (see page 38).

Scabiosa (Dipsacaceae) The scabious or pincushion flower belongs to a genus of 100 species of annual and herbaceous perennials. The daisy-like flowers cut well, and dry and dye well too. The slightly unfortunate name does indeed refer to scabies, the Latin word for itch, as it was thought the plant could cure the skin disease.

Sea Grape, see **Coccoloba**

Seaweed I used some hardened whirls of a seaweed from South Africa in the Bermudan step-by-step arrangement. This was soft, obviously, when collected, but became hard and black as it dried. Because it could soften again, it must be kept away from water. I once saw some being used in a show arrangement, *in* water, and long before the judges arrived it had collapsed! There are similar seaweeds in Europe which can be used this way, particularly channelled wrack and sea thongs. Other 'sea weeds' are the sea ferns found on beaches in the Caribbean. These dry well, some actually encrusted with coral and looking like a lichened branch.

Sedum (Crassulaceae) A genus of about 600 species of annuals and perennials, deciduous and evergreen succulents, which can be garden, greenhouse or pot grown. A number are mat-forming, thus the common names of stone crop or gold moss,

and the official one – coming from the Latin *sedere*, to sit. Many have attractive flowers and leaf shapes.

Snowberry, see **Symphoricarpos**

Solidago (Compositae) Goldenrod belongs to a genus of 100 species of herbaceous perennials, native originally to North America. The plumes of clustered yellow flowers cut well and are very effective in flower arrangements. The name is said to come from the Latin *solido*, to make whole, referring to the medicinal properties of some species.

Sorbus (Rosaceae) A genus of 100 species of deciduous trees and shrubs with hawthorn-like flowers and berries, native to many temperate zones. *S. aucuparia*, the rowan or mountain ash, is so useful as a foliage, both for its good colour-changing leaves and for its berries, bright orangey red. (Try to beat the birds to them.)

Spathiphyllum (Araceae) A genus of over 30 evergreen perennial greenhouse and pot plants, native to tropical America, particularly Colombia. They are related to the anthurium lily (see page 127), but are more easily grown. They have bright shiny green lanceolate leaves and small flowers in a spike emerging from a white spathe shaped rather like an arum. The name comes from the

Greek *spathe*, spathe, and *phyllon*, leaf.

Stephanandra (Rosaceae) A genus of four species of flowering shrubs native to Japan and Korea. The graceful and tinted autumn foliage is very useful in many arrangements.

Symphoricarpos (Caprifoliaceae) A genus of 18 species of berry-bearing shrubs native to North America. The plants bear small flowers before the berries, white on the *S. albus*, the snowberry (or, as it's called in the States, the mothball bush), pink on *S. orbiculatus*, coral berry or Indian currant. The berries persist, so foliage is useful in autumn and winter arrangements. The name comes from the Greek *symphonein*, bear together, and *karpos*, fruit.

Ulmus (Ulmaceae) The elm tree belongs to a genus of 45 species of deciduous trees native mainly to Europe. The bright green leaves of some varieties turn deep yellow in the autumn or winter. Green or yellow sprays make good flower-arranging foliage, and interesting green-winged fruits develop as the leaves unfold.

Wattle, see **Acacia**

Weigela (Caprifoliaceae) A genus of 12 species of flowering shrubs native to China and Japan. The small foxglove-type flowers are borne in clusters. The ovate leaves are light

green and wrinkled, borne on arching branches: *W. florida* 'Variegata' has yellow margined leaves. It was named after a German botanist, Christian Ehrenfeld Weigel.

Willow, see **Salix**

Wineberry, *see* **Rubus**

Yucca (Agavaceae) A genus of about 40 species of stemless or erect woody-stemmed plants with long strap-shaped leaves in a loose rosette. They are native to the south-eastern USA, but can grow in European gardens, and are also available as house plants. Outdoor plants can produce flowers when they are three to five years old. Other common names for the plants are Spanish bayonet or needle, Adam's needle and dagger plant. The leaves can be variegated, and they can be dried successfully.

INDEX

Page numbers in *italic* denote illustrations.